MW01254960

BANGIN'
THE MAKING OF A Y.G.

Jonas Royster

PARADISE
PUBLISHING COMPANY

Bangin' The Making of A Y.G. by Jonas Royster
Published by Paradise Publishing Company
www.paradisepublishingcompany.com

The following is a work of fiction. Names, characters, places, and incidents are the product of the author's imagination or are used fictitiously. Any resemblance to actual events, locales, or persons, living or dead, is coincidental.

All rights reserved. No portion of this book may be reproduced in any form without permission from the publisher, except as permitted by U.S. copyright law. For permissions contact:
info@paradisepublishingcompany.com

Copyright © 2021 Jonas Royster
Art Direction by Davelle.com
Cover Art by BoxOfWolves.com
Copy editing & line editing by Lisa Royster
Developmental editing by Vera Sanchez

ISBN: 978-0-578-89034-0

Printed in United States of America
First Edition
Jonas Royster
8456 Mira Loma Ave.
Hemet, CA, 92545
paradisepublishingcompany@gmail.com

Much Luv 2 My Luv 1's

My fondest memories were the spring days of junior high when Alex, Lee and I would sneak over Mrs. White's fence and fill our backpacks up with her loquats that never seemed to spoil. I remember one year, I think it was the day before April fools that Mrs. White caught us all picking from her tree, Lee and I made a quick escape back over the fence but Alex wasn't so lucky. Mrs. White beat him with her walking cane like he was stealing her last hundred dollar bill. As we ran down the block to our houses we could hear Alex hollering for her to stop. The laughter that ensued had my stomach hurting later that night as I ate my loquats on my bed and watched Wonder Years.

My pops almost sideswiped a family of four in their Mercedes Benz as he merged the beat-up U Haul onto the freeway. Ahead of us in the distance, I could see the flags of all 32 NFL teams blowing in the wind on top of Qualcomm Stadium. As we passed by I realized my pops and I bi-weekly trips to the stadium to watch Drew Brees and LaDainian Tomlinson lead the San Diego Chargers to victories were going to become obsolete and so was our Saturday morning film sessions of my varsity football games.

When my dad blew his knee his junior year at SDSU his football dreams were cut short but that never diminished his love for the game. Every Saturday morning at 9 am like clockwork he would break down film with me from my varsity football game the night before. We'd sit in the man cave he built in the spacious two-car garage that sat overlooking the Point Loma Yacht Club.

He always preached for me to go after my dreams but "don't be foolish, make sure you have a backup plan." He would say, "If you fail to plan you plan to fail." That mantra in his life was what had us living, at the time, in a 3,000 square foot home in Point Loma. His backup plan of becoming an engineer worked out perfectly.

The same passion and commitment he invested on the football field he did the same at his job. My pops went to work faithfully, every morning at 4:30 am. On occasions, I would catch him peek his head into my room and check on me before he headed off to work. He took pride in being the first in the doors and the last one out. He told me in the 17 years of working at General Dynamics that he only missed one day of work and that was because I didn't listen and I had to pop my head out my moms "glove box", as he liked to call it and enter the world on Friday, December 6th, 1980 instead of Saturday as he had planned.

Deshaun

Chapter 1

———•••———

Driving past the military barracks on Rosecrans heading to the 8 East freeway in a bite-size U-Haul squished in between my pops tree trunk of an arm and my mom's gigantic bosom I felt like I was going to suffocate, literally. I couldn't believe my pops lost his job and we had to leave everything I've ever known, and what made it worse was that we had to move across town, to the southeast.

My whole seventeen years of life were spent right there in Point Loma exploring every nook and cranny that my neighborhood had to offer. From the cookie-cutter houses with the manicured front lawns and pristine housewives to the lavender leaf Jacaranda trees that line every block and always seemed to be in full bloom.

My neighborhood was a spitting image of my favorite television show. I remembered my elementary days were spent climbing those same Jacaranda trees and hiding myself in its purple clouds to escape the evil invaders (adults as I like to call them now) that roamed the sidewalks.

wanted to return to my room for the rest of the summer. I didn't want to make new friends if this was the way to go about it. I knew I was on his turf and had to respect the rules of the neighborhood but damn. Meeting people wasn't this important to me.

"You bang?"

"Nah," I get now why he was so adamant. My lame-ass didn't understand what he was asking. He was just checking to see if I was from the other side of town, making sure I wasn't an enemy or a buster trying to infiltrate. As we arrived at the park, it was filled with a gang of heads. Half of them looked like they were jacked up on steroids, while the other half was draped in red and burgundy clothing. I sensed Pernell knew I was uneasy about the situation.

"Don't act scared now. Them just the homies right there." Not wanting to give much eye contact, I gave a slight head nod to acknowledge everyone standing in front of me. Pernell introduced me to everyone, like in the movie the Sandlot when Benny "the Jet" Rodriguez, introduces Smalls to his baseball crew. Pernell pointed to a buff looking dude with a devil-horned bitch tatted on his forearm. "That's Arm & Hammer. Blood got the meanest knuckle game I know." Arm & Hammer looked like he could give two fucks that Pernell just complimented his fighting skills. He ignored the comment and focused his attention on some dude standing next to me.

Arm & Hammer's bald head shined as if he buffed it out with Turtle Wax before he came outside. The beads of sweat that were developing over his brow made it hard as hell to get a gauge on his intent, his stare was colder than a seal's pussy. I tried not to stare too hard but the veins that were protruding from his forearm and his neck made him seem like a freak of nature. I couldn't tell if his physique was country fed or steroid-induced but what I did know was he resembled a teenage Bo Jackson and I wanted no part.

"The homie right there smoking the blunt," Pernell gestured to a lanky guy standing off to my right. The aroma from his blunt smelled like he rolled up a dead skunk. His marble black skin blended perfectly with his black shirt. "That's Slim."

Slim took a step closer and extended his arm. "You wanna hit this?"

Knowing I needed to be on my p's and q's, I respectfully declined.

Pernell laughed, "Good choice. He's been smoking the older homies under the table for years." Pernell rejected the blunt as well, "His pops is tied in with the Jamaicans, so he's been blowing trees since he was seven."

Slim nodded and handed the blunt to a kid who looked no more than fourteen years of age. The young man's caramel complexion was smooth, not a hint of peach fuzz lined his face, and he couldn't be taller than five feet, but his swag was on point. The burgundy Adidas tracksuit he wore with the mustard lines down the side resembled the Washington Redskins colors.

"The kid smoking the blunt, that's the young homie, Fly."

Fly blew a giant ring of smoke my way. "What's brackin', homie?" Fly passed the blunt back to Slim. "Don't listen to anything blood is telling you. Until he can get his swag up, everything he has to say is outdated like that fit he has on." Fly joked about Pernell, but that shit quickly turned bad.

"Check this out. Watch your smart ass mouth when you talkin. I'm your big homie, not some little nigga you be playing with at lunchtime." The seriousness in Pernell's voice made me erase the smile off my face. I didn't need him thinking I was siding with Fly or anyone else for that matter.

Pernell refocused his attention on me, "He got some nerve talking to me like that. Everyone knows that as soon as he gets tackled, he finna start crying. Just make sure you ready for the ass whooping ya momma finna give you for fucking up your school clothes."

Pernell continued giving me the rundown on everyone at the park, but I found myself staring back at Arm & Hammer, trying not to be obvious about it. He still had his eye on that same dude. It felt like I was watching a lion stalk a gazelle. If my memory was correct, Pernell said his name was Buster Rob. Arm & Hammer effortlessly positioned himself to the right of Buster Rob. I could see Arm & Hammer's pupils darting from left to right before he pivoted his right foot and exploded through Buster Rob's chin. Buster Rob's knees buckled, and his head hung forward like a limp flower, as his chin sat on his chest. He was crumbling fast, but Arm & Hammer wanted one last punch. He executed a right cross to Buster Rob's temple, making his head look like it was about to snap in half. His body stiffened like a plank board before he hit the concrete. Arm & Hammer stood over the body.

"Fuck you, you snitch ass nigga!" Arm & Hammer drew his foot as far back as he could and booted Buster

He gave General Dynamics everything he had and at times it seemed like he gave them a little more than he did my mom and I. His eight-hour shifts routinely became twelve and when my mom would ask him why he gave them so much of his time his response was always the same, "Now, Jennifer, you know that if you only put a little bit in you will only get a little bit out but if you put a whole lot in then you will get a whole lot back out."

By the time we exited the freeway, it felt like there was a cosmic shift in the universe. All the colors seemed to vanish, our new surroundings felt like a concrete jungle. The Jacaranda trees that lined the streets of my old neighborhood were now replaced with splintered telephone poles with Chuck Taylors thrown over the lines. Every building had iron wrought security bars around their windows and padded gates, it reminded me of my Uncle Juney's neck of the woods.

My dad's brother Juney stayed on 41st and Raven. From age twelve to sixteen my mom routinely dropped me off at his house during the summer. She told me I needed to "toughen" up but I never really understood what she meant. I mean there was never a time I got picked on while I was at school and when I did get in a couple of fights it was because someone called me a nigger in class and please believe I made sure I whooped their ass so bad that their mamma could feel it.

My pops made a left onto Alta View Dr. and crossed the threshold of the broken security gate of the apartments. The manilla stucco building with the dookie brown trimming seemed like its better days were long and gone. Pops swung the U-Haul into our parking space, number 228. Even though we had to downsize and had gotten the smallest U-Haul truck known to mankind, our parking spot looked like it was made for a kid's Power Wheel.

Looking at all the surrounding apartment buildings in this complex everything felt so compacted, so drawn into each other. There wasn't much space for a kid to do anything around here. Two buildings to the east of where we were parked were a large group of kids congregating around a green electrical box that sat in front of the building in an open area of grass. The group mostly consisted of boys but there were also girls, and girls that dressed like boys. Age didn't seem to matter much either, from my vantage point in the U-Haul but it looked like three of the boys should've been in someone's kindergarten class and not hanging out on some green box. Clouds of smoke hovered over the group as I watched them pass blunts and brews one after another in a clockwise rotation.

My mom must've seen what I saw and tapped me on my shoulder and pointed out her window. "Son, you see all those boys in red over there," I looked past her outstretched arm acting like I hadn't already seen them. "Don't let me catch you hanging out with them, you hear me? Nothing good comes from young black boys hanging out on a green box. Ask your Uncle Juney." As my pops moved the giant lever into park position the knuckleheads posted on the block slowly turned our way, making it obvious we were new to the neighborhood and not welcome. I was too scared to stare back, so I just looked forward to the apartment wall in front of us. First rules in the hood: mind your damn business and never snitch. It seemed simple enough, right? But surprisingly, you never know who's watching and who's gonna switch. Everyone is a suspect, even the ones closest to you.

Chapter 2

My summer days started off boring since I was new to the neighborhood. I found myself writing in my journal more and more, reminiscing on the times Alex, Lee and I found ourselves in trouble stealing fruit from the neighbor's trees. That's the most trouble I've gotten into. I knew moving wouldn't be easy, and I was initially happy to leave Point Loma. Man, was I wrong. Most of my days I spent locked up in my room feeling sorry for myself and moms began to worry. She would come to check on me throughout the day making sure I was fed, fixing me simple meals like a grilled cheese sandwich or a quesadilla. She never asked me specifically if there was anything wrong, but I could tell by the look in her eyes that she was worried about me. But my lonely summer days changed the day I met Pernell.

When the doorbell rang, I peeked out my window and caught a glimpse of a boy standing at our door. I could hear my mother's high pitched voice reassuring the young man, "You didn't bother us. Let me see if he's up." Moms was always polite whenever guests came over the pad, but her high pitched voice quickly turned piercing when she spoke to me, "Deshaun, get 'cha ass up and out that room. There's some boy at the door for you." I threw my journal on my bed and slipped on my shoes. My sweatsuit didn't match, but I didn't care much. I just wanted to figure out who was at our door.

"Who is it?" I yelled back, forgetting my manners.

"Boy, getcha ass out here and quit yelling. You need to get out of this house and put some sun on that yellow ass, anyways."

When I reached the front door, I gave my mom a kiss on her cheek and apologized for my rudeness. She rubbed her hand through my curls and smiled, a sign of affection that she accepted my apology. The butterflies in my stomach started to soar as I opened the door. Meeting new people was never my strong suit, but moms' was right. It was about time I got to know the neighborhood and meet some new friends.

"What's up?" was all I heard as I swung the door wide open. The person in front of me sort of resembled Alex. The tone on his athletic frame was a shade darker than a pinecone, and his waves looked like he layered them with a gallon of Murray's. He was no taller than a college running back and his beady black eyes looked like they lost their soul years ago. His Kodak smile made me subconscious about the braces I knew I needed.

"Who are you?"

"You Deshaun, right? I saw you move in a couple of weeks back." I tried to jog my memory when I saw him, but couldn't. "I live right there," he pointed to the apartment directly across the courtyard, "My name Pernell. We got a pick up game of smear the queer set up at the park if you wanna come through."

"Hell yeah, I do," I replied as my eyes lit up. Football was what I lived for, and I couldn't turn down the opportunity. Since I was in my room all summer, this was the perfect time for me to let out my aggression and run it up on dudes. Pernell grinned. He must've thought since I weighed only a buck twenty, dripping wet, that I couldn't ball. He nodded his head for me to follow him, and he laughed as he went down the stairs.

Following Pernell down the snake-like sidewalk to the park I felt like a fish in a fishbowl and everyone's eyes in the apartments were on me. I didn't actually see anybody watching me but I could feel their eyes stabbing me with suspicion. As we got closer to the park, smells that were foreign in my old neighborhood now bombarded my nostrils. If it wasn't for all the hotboxes I walked through at my Uncle Juney's house, I would've thought there was a dead skunk lying close by. With a couple more steps that stark pine needle stench started to blend with a sweet smell that reminded me of our vacation to Mexico City. It brought me back to the uneven brick road where my parents and I sat on a splintered wooden bench and ate fresh tortillas made by the town's abuelita.

As we got closer to the "park," I realized it wasn't really a park at all. It was just a circular area no bigger than an elementary school's blacktop. The grass that was still alive looked like peach fuzz sprinkled on the dirt lot. I smiled and chuckled to myself. I could now see how I was gonna run these dudes up and down this field. Highlights of me catching passes like Shawn Jefferson kept flashing across my mind.

Pernell stopped to look at me, "What the fuck is so funny?"

"Noth-," Pernell didn't even let me finish my words.

"So, Deshaun," Pernell's demeanor started to shift, "where you use to stay at?" Pernell's question threw me for a loop as I noticed his fist start to ball up.

Answering, like a simple square, I blurted out the truth, "In Point Loma."

The muscles in Pernell's jaw looked like he was chewing boulders, "Don't lie to me. You lookin' real familiar right now."

"What are you talk-" he interrupted me again.

"What school you go to?"

"Francis Parker." I wanted to say it sarcastically, like where the fuck else would I go? I mean, it wasn't rocket science, and anyone with common sense would know if you lived in Point Loma you went to a private school. But, I quickly learned that Pernell was not the one to say something smart to or else it would be my ass.

Pernell squinted, making it impossible to see his pupils. White spittle formed on the side of his mouth. "Where the fuck is you from, blood?"

Where were all these random questions coming from? He was asking more questions than a nosey girlfriend. It made me feel uncomfortable, and I

Rob's head. "You thought I was finna let that shit slide?" Buster Rob's eyes rolled into the back of his head and his body laid lifeless on the sidewalk. It was like blood was in the ocean and a frenzy of sharks surrounded the wounded animal. Muthafuckas were even pushing each other out the way so they could get their kicks in. I'd only seen shit like that in movies I watched with Uncle Juney. The pure disregard for human life was in full display, and I can bet that no one there would've given a fuck if Buster Rob lived or died. I wanted to jump in and tell them all to stop. I felt helpless not doing anything, but I knew that's what I had to do to survive in this neighborhood.

Before you know it, wailing screams of police sirens brought everything back into perspective, and by the time I looked for Pernell, he was gone. I watched a crowd scattering throughout the streets and back alleys, everyone going in their own direction. It seemed like everyone had their own path sketched out like they had done this before. I didn't know where to run, but I had to make a decision soon. I knew if I was caught by Buster Rob's body, I was gonna be the one charged with an assault.

"Deshaun," Pernell's voice was off in the distance, "over here."

I scanned the park to see if I could see him but saw nothing. The sirens were growing louder, and it sounded like more than one car now.

"Pernell, where the fuck are you?" I finally yelled out, spinning myself in a circle.

"Behind the flame Chevy. Hurry the fuck up!" The red Chevy was parked next to a huge F-250 in a parking lot about a hundred yards away. Michael Johnson must've been my distant relative because that was the fastest I had ever ran in life. Pernell's outfit blended perfectly with the color of the Chevy, which is why I had a hard time spotting him.

Pernell rose up to peek over the roof of the Chevy. "They ain't here yet. Let's get the fuck outta here."

Sprinting behind Pernell through the apartments, all I could think about was that ass whooping they gave Buster Rob. The images of Arm & Hammer sucker-punching Buster Rob flashed through my head like some kind of action movie. I tried to shake off the image, but it was no use. I knew I would go to bed tonight thinking about Buster Rob and if he survived.

After running for a few minutes, we finally reached the apartment. I was able to rest my hands on my knees to catch my breath, "Good looking back there. Thanks for not leaving me for the dead."

Pernell pulled his Dickies up, without saying a word, and stood inches from my face. His beady, black eyes stared directly through me. "Don't you ever use my muthafuckin' government name again." I tried to recall when I used his name since everything happened so quickly, but my brain was drawing a blank, and then it hit me.

"My bad, bro."

Pernell didn't bat an eye over my apology, "This is your one pass on this shit. You do some shit like that again, and I'ma do you how the homie just did Buster Rob."

I nodded my head in agreement. "What should I call you, then?"

The corners of Pernell's mouth curled upwards like the Joker's and his eyes brightened, "Call me Y.A."

"Y.A.?" I asked, unsure that I heard him correctly.

"Yea, nigga, Young muthafuckin' Active." Once again, Pernell blew off my sentiments and looked at his watch. "I'm finna go check out this bitch. I'll get identify the police. It was all new to me, so I wrote the words and definitions in my journal so that I wouldn't forget, like if I was preparing to take a vocabulary test at school, only this wasn't for a grade. This was for survival.

I remember the day Pernell gave me a crash course on how to steal some "drank" from the neighborhood grocery store. We were on our usual trip to the store to stock up for the day when Pernell switched up the routine, "I know you usually wait outside and catch my back fade, but today it's your turn to jack a bottle. Everyone in there already knows my face. Don't nobody know yours." My heart dropped to the cement as he uttered these words to me. The back of my neck started to heat up and beads of sweat started to form around my upper lip. I ain't never stole anything in my life other than loquats with Alex and Lee. And even stealing fruit from someone's yard made me feel guilty for a whole week. It never bothered me drinking the liquor Pernell stole, but as far as me stealing and risking my freedom, that was another story, and a for sure ass whooping if I got caught.

Pernell sensed my reluctance and spoke up,"Whatchu scared for? We do this shit every day and don't nothing happen to me." He was right. For my knees to catch my breath, "Good looking back there. Thanks for not leaving me for the dead."

Pernell pulled his Dickies up, without saying a word, and stood inches from my face. His beady, black eyes stared directly through me. "Don't you ever use my muthafuckin' government name again." I tried to recall when I used his name since everything happened so quickly, but my brain was drawing a blank, and then it hit me.

"My bad, bro."

Pernell didn't bat an eye over my apology, "This is your one pass on this shit. You do some shit like that again, and I'ma do you how the homie just did Buster Rob."

I nodded my head in agreement. "What should I call you, then?"

The corners of Pernell's mouth curled upwards like the Joker's and his eyes brightened, "Call me Y.A."

"Y.A.?" I asked, unsure that I heard him correctly.

"Yea, nigga, Young muthafuckin' Active." Once again, Pernell blew off my sentiments and looked at his watch. "I'm finna go check out this bitch. I'll get with'cha tomorrow." Pernell gave me a dap before he walked up the stairs and left me standing in the courtyard by myself. I had to gather my emotions before going back home. Moms always had a sharp intuition, so I was hoping I could play it off when I entered the house. Luckily for me, she was at the store buying groceries for dinner. She left a note on the refrigerator door saying that she would be back by 5:30 p.m. and to have my appetite ready after a long day of playing football. This gave me time to make up a story about how my team beat Pernell's team in a friendly game of smear the queer. I quickly ran to my room, grabbed my journal, and jotted down what had just occurred. I would later ask Uncle Juney about the unwritten rules of the hood. You see, when shit goes down, you react and ask questions later or better yet you don't ask questions at all. If this was the beginning of my summer, I can only imagine how the rest of it was going to play out.

Chapter 3

—◆••◆—

Spending time with my dad started to become more of a memory than reality. It didn't matter how late I stayed up waiting for him to come to my room and check on me in the middle of the night. He never came. Even when I was asleep, I had trained my ear to listen when my eyes were closed. I practiced this every night, listening to his work boots tiptoeing through the living room, his work bag placed on the kitchen table, pops brushing his teeth before he went to bed, and the sighs of his breath from being overworked before he shut his eyes only to repeat the next morning.

It didn't take much for me to seek attention elsewhere. Over the next month, Pernell and I became thick as thieves. There wasn't a day that went by that someone wouldn't see the two of us together. Even though I was a year older, he seemed like a big brother to me. His knowledge of the streets was immense and I was a sponge soaking up all that I could, teaching me the rules of the streets; What to look out for, what to say, the proper jargon the police used versus the slang in the hood. The only time I heard the word babylon was in a Bob Marley song. I had no clue it was to identify the police. It was all new to me, so I wrote the words and definitions in my journal so that I wouldn't forget, like if I was preparing to take a vocabulary test at school, only this wasn't for a grade. This was for survival.

I remember the day Pernell gave me a crash course on how to steal some "drank" from the neighborhood grocery store. We were on our usual trip to the store to stock up for the day when Pernell switched up the routine, "I know you usually wait outside and catch my back fade, but today it's your turn to jack a bottle. Everyone in there already knows my face. Don't nobody know yours." My heart dropped to the cement as he uttered these words to me. The back of my neck started to heat up and beads of sweat started to form around my upper lip. I ain't never stole anything in my life other than loquats with Alex and Lee. And even stealing fruit from someone's yard made me feel guilty for a whole week. It never bothered me drinking the liquor Pernell stole, but as far as me stealing and risking my freedom, that was another story, and a for sure ass whooping if I got caught.

Pernell sensed my reluctance and spoke up, "Whatchu scared for? We do this shit every day and don't nothing happen to me." He was right. For the last ten days, not a single soul followed him out. He continued, "All you have to do is walk along the back of the store, past the meat section and the liquor aisle will be on your right. Grab the bottle, stuff that muthafucka, and walk out." Pernell reached in his pocket and pulled out a scratch piece of paper, "Look, I even drew a map for you of the store layout in case you forget my directions." He patted me on my back as I pulled my jeans over my butt and tightened my belt. Pernell knew how to boost my confidence in a matter of seconds. "And look my nigga, if anyone tries to snatch you up I got chu, on the set." His words dripped with confidence as he tangled his fingers to form a letter of a 'P'. I didn't want to disappoint him so I nodded, clutching the paper, and headed inside.

As I walked to the back of the store as outlined on the scratch paper, the bright fluorescents that hung over my head made me feel like I was on a Broadway stage with all eyes on me. By the time I passed the meat department, the liquor aisle was in near sight. I quickly glanced to my left and noticed the butcher was busy cutting a thick piece of marbleized meat for a young pastor and his wife. The pastor and his wife were dressed in their best Sunday clothing, the pastor wearing his pressed jacket with the platinum cross dangling from his neck, and his wife wearing those Easter type hats with a bunch of flowers decorated on it.

It's clear, I thought to myself. Walking towards the liquor aisle, I now understood why Pernell liked jacking drank from a grocery store rather than a liquor store. There were hundreds of choices within arms reach, and no one to stop him from picking one up and walking out. Scanning the isle, my eyes caught a glimpse of a bottle with a long red stem and matching cap. On the label, it read Bacardi 151. It was the perfect size to tuck in my waist. I quickly grabbed the bottle and ripped off the security label on the bottom, stuffing it in my jeans. When I looked around, there was not a soul in sight even though I had an eerie feeling that I was being watched or maybe it was my conscience playing with my head.

Making my way back to the front of the store I could hardly walk straight. I did my best not to stick my hands down my pants to adjust the bottle pressing against my nuts. I continued to scan the people in the store. Everyone was too busy minding their own business to even notice me. Sometimes living in the hood has its advantages. People here are trained to stick to themselves. If it doesn't involve them, it doesn't matter. In the hood, nobody respects a snitch. It was way different from living in Point Loma where every block conducted their own neighborhood watch meeting held the third Wednesday of the month to review safety tips and procedures. White people voted on assignments while drinking vanilla latte in their backyard as their kids played Marco Polo in the swimming pool.

As I stepped closer to the sliding glassdoor, my confidence began to grow. I knew Pernell would be proud of me once I showed him I was down for the set. This would be the first street test I passed with flying colors. This test meant more to me than any of the straight A's I earned on my report card just to please my pops. That is until I felt a heavy paw land on my right shoulder and pull me back. The smell of black licorice reeking from his pores was a dead giveaway, and I knew exactly who that paw belonged to. It was the oversized Russian security guard nicknamed the Giant. Pernell mentioned him in previous trips to the grocery store, but I never thought much of it because Pernall was never caught. The Giant's body was both swollen with muscle and fat, and his pointy teeth seemed ready to tear into my flesh.

"Get off me," I squirmed, kicking his tree sized leg, but it didn't phase him one bit. His laugh echoed as if it came from inside a cave, and he threw me over his shoulder like a sack of rice. "Let me fucking go! I ain't got shit!" I tried headbutting him this time, but the Giant's laugh only grew louder with every attempt I tried to escape. Now, everyone who was minding their own business turned their attention towards me, including the pastor and his wife, who raised their hands and prayed to thy Lord to save my soul from evil. The Giant dangled me all the way to the manager's door that led to the upstairs interrogation room. As he opened the door, all I could imagine was the ass whooping my moms was going to give me once she picked me up from the police station. Before the Giant took another step up the stairs his legs were swept from under him and we both fell. Luckily, I was over his shoulder and his face became my cushion as I landed, the bottle rolling from the bottom of my jeans. Blood quickly filled the steps of the staircase, the Giant throwing his hands over his nose and screamed a word that only Mikhail Gorbachev would've understood.

Hurrying to get up, I heard Pernell's voice over all the commotion. "Let's go, blood!" Pernell grabbed the back of my white tee and pulled me through the door. We both ran out the store but not before I picked up the bottle from the floor to complete my mission. We ran all the way back to the apartments, dodging cars, ignoring street lights and shoving through pedestrians during their afternoon walk. This is where all those football drills and sprints came into play. The conditioning, hitting the pads, pushing myself during the final minutes of the game seemed like real life.

As we got to the stairs of the apartment, Pernell grabbed the bottle from my hand, "I told you I got chu." He popped open the bottle and took a long swig. "You did good today, young nigga," he took another gulp before handing the bottle back to me. I followed his lead, wiping my mouth after drinking my share of the alcohol. There, in front of the stairs, we finished the bottle until it was gone. By this time, the pounding from my heart had settled down and I was able to enjoy my buzz for the rest of the afternoon. I looked over at Pernell who was tilting his head towards the sky. I didn't know what he was thinking at that moment, but I knew deep down I had earned his respect, even though Pernell wasn't much for kind words. He showed me that he had my back and in return, I was going to show him that I had his. From that day forward, I forgot my pops' words to me and trusted everything Pernell had to say.

Chapter 4

It wasn't like all of this should be completely new to me. After all, I had watched enough television to know how shit goes down if you try to steal something from a store. Take the movie, *Menace to Society*, for example. The opening scene where Caine and O-Dog went into the liquor store for their drank and came out as an accessory to murder and armed robbery. Although Pernell and I didn't kill anyone, we still left the grocery store with a case, and that would be enough for two young black kids to be tried as adults and do time in juvy. I later thought about the cameras and how I could easily be identified by the babylons. That night I didn't get much sleep. My conscience kept eating me alive and all I could do was hear moms' voice in my head. How disappointed in me she was or how I should focus on my studies instead of running around with the neighborhood knuckleheads. I did my best to cover up the times I came home faded and hid the bruises I had from falling on the Giant. It felt like my right arm was connected to a live wire, the way the pain was shooting from my shoulder to the tips of my fingers. The tingling sensation felt like a thousand

29

needles were pricking my skin. This feeling reminded me of a stinger I received in a playoff football game last year, luckily, I knew how to patch up my injuries.

I grabbed the Icy Hot that I kept in my top drawer and took a giant scoop with my fingers and slabbed it across my right shoulder down the length of my arm. I scooted down to the foot of my bed so I could examine my arm in the mirror. My arm hung against the side of my body like a limp twig and I could hardly lift it above my chest. If pops was around, he would've noticed something was suspicious. He would've pulled up my shirt to prove his instincts were right. Pops could spot an injury a mile away, part of his training in the Navy. Even if he did notice, I would come up with a lie, how I got injured playing tackle football at the park. It wouldn't even be that far of a stretch considering I was tackled, with the bottle as my football. Leaving the grocery store with the bottle was like crossing the goal line and scoring a game-winning touchdown, Pernell being my main blocker.

As I rubbed my hand along my arm, I sensed someone's heavy steps from outside. One of the things that sucked about living in these apartments was that everything was so poorly constructed. The walls were so thin you could hear the neighbors either fucking or arguing and the floors felt like they were made with one sheet of plywood. Anytime anyone walked along the outside of our front door, it felt like tiny earthquake aftershocks reverberated throughout my bedroom. At least for us, it was only me, moms and pops in our apartment. Other apartments had at least six to seven heads living in a one-bedroom with kids sleeping on the living room floor because their parents couldn't afford a bed.

Before the Icy Hot went into its full effect, there was once again that familiar tap outside my bedroom window. Over the last month, it became routine.

"Get cha ass up, nigga. We finna smash to the mall." Little did Pernell know I had been up all night no thanks to him. I wouldn't dare ask him questions about the cameras or if he suspected the babylons were on a search hunt for us. I didn't want to look like a buster after our big score. I placed the Icy Hot back in my dresser and hid it underneath my wife beaters.

"Hold up. I'll get with you in a minute," I said after I slid open my window.

"What's wrong with you? Don't tell me you're injured from yesterday," Pernell smirked as he rubbed his chin. Fuck. Pernell might as well be my dad since he had an eye for spotting any wrongdoing. No wonder all his homies respected him. He was smarter than all of them. If Pernell wasn't so hood, he could easily be a P.I. or work for the FBI solving crimes. He may only be 16 and a half years old, but he had the wisdom of an older sensei.

"Don't worry, young buck. I won't tell the rest of the homies you almost got hemmed up at the store. Hide da Icy Hot from your moms and hurry your ass up. We got more shit to do today. I'm finna teach you how to hop the trolley."

***

The city bus dropped Pernell and I off on Imperial Ave right across the street from Salaam's Fish House. The smell of red snapper fillets mixed with flour and hot oil stimulated my nostrils. It reminded me of the fish frying at Uncle Juney's house, where my pops and his brother used their hands like spatulas to retrieve the cooked fillets out of the cast-iron caldron that sat on an open flame in the kitchen. Through the chain-link fence, I saw that the trolley station was packed with all sorts of people from the elder Ethiopians to the homeless vet carrying his American flag and cardboard sign. My eyes jumped from groups of people congregating to solo patrons minding their own business, my ears picking up the rhythmic flow of conversation.

But what caught my attention the most was the sexiest Latina I have ever seen since I watched Rosie Perez in *White Men Can't Jump*. Her lightly curled hair floated on top of her exposed clavicles, while her grapefruit-size breasts were fighting hard to bust out of her one size too small white halter top. I felt my dick starting to get hard until Pernell interrupted.

"Them muthafuckas know who to fuck with."

He nudged me, and my eyes were diverted to a group of South Siders no older than us. They were patting the pockets of a white kid who looked like he regretted getting off at the wrong stop. His plain white collar shirt and navy blue clip-on tie hung over his khaki dockers. All four of his pockets looked like bunny ears, and two South Siders, or as Pernell called them "*eses*," were rummaging through the white kid's Jansport backpack. Pernell nodded his head in their direction as we walked past them on our way to the end of the platform.

Once we walked past them, my attention veered back to the Rosie Perez *mamacita*. Her dimples deepened as she popped her gum, and I imagined her full lips kissing my most intimate body parts. I started to get hard again, but again, my fantasies were interrupted by Pernell, who noticed her too. He began walking towards her, his strides getting longer as he approached. Before I knew it, his smooth voice was already whispering in her ear and she began to giggle, playfully slapping him on his arm. Her once standoffish attitude slowly began to soften as Pernell took out a black ballpoint pen from his pocket and began to write her phone number on the palm of his hand.

"You smell so good," Pernell placed his nose against her neck, "what chu wearin'?"

"Very Sexy by Victoria Secret. It was my birthday present," Mamacita responded.

"If you were my girl, I'd buy you all the Very Sexy perfume you desired." Pernell stuck his hands in his pocket and flashed Mamacita a stack of twenty-dollar bills. He rubbed his nose down the length of her neck and pressed himself against her breast.

"Aye, puto! What the fuck do you think you're doing with my girl, holmes?" I turned around and saw the same group of *ese's* walking aggressively our way. "She doesn't talk to mayates, so back the fuck up!" Another *ese* shouted, who was covered in old English tattoos. Pernell didn't break stride. He finished writing her phone number on his palm and planted a kiss on her cheek.

Like always, I began to panic inside, and the pit of my stomach dropped as my knees began to shake. But Pernell, he was ready for any situation at any given time. Pernell drew the red Franklin gloves that always hung halfway out his back pocket.

"Get ready, my nigga," Pernell said as he put his gloves on, "it's finna get brackin'." Pernell took a giant step towards the *eses* that were approaching us. The smile on his face showed his confidence as he kept punching his right fist into his left hand. "Now which one of you bitch ass Mexicans wanna get knocked out first?"

Before I could pull up my pants, Pernell dropped the first *ese* that ran up on him. The *ese* melted into the sidewalk as if his soul was snatched from his body as his jawline laid flat on the cement. I've never seen a one-hitter-quitter in a street fight. Pernell always had a way of surprising me every time we hung out. The people at the trolley stop formed a circle around us, their cheers only egging us on, and I quickly lost sight of Mamacita. My stomach now shifted to uneasiness as I knew it was my turn to perform. Problem was I didn't have hands like Pernell.

I closed my eyes and started swinging, waiting for the inevitable. Either it was going to be my fist connecting to someone's chin or it was going to be me waking up next to the *ese* that Pernell dropped.

By the time I opened my eyes, it was Pernell, me, and only one *ese* left standing. The look in his eyes gleamed of defeat, but his pride kept him standing like a warrior in his last battle. Pernell and I surrounded him and inched our way closer. The *ese's* pride turned into worry as the rest of his homies struggled to get up and help. My ears detected a sound coming from behind Pernell and I. The jingling of what sounded like brass keys slapping against one another were approaching fast.

"Them people is coming, fam," a voice from the crowd shouted. As I turned to see who was coming from behind, the *ese* took his opportunity and sprinted across the trolley tracks, hopping the chain link fence. Pernell already knew the drill, shoving his way through the crowd, who were already imitating his one-hitter quitter and cheering as he escaped from another crime scene. For a minute, I stood there in shock. My mind screamed to run but my body stayed still. Yesterday was theft; today was battery. It was only a matter of time before something more serious would come. Then, I heard Pernell's voice trailing in the distance.

"We gotta make it back to the set!"

Chapter 5

———•••———

We ran all the way back to a house that I wasn't familiar with and the garage door was already open. Every time we got into some shit, he always seemed casual after, like nothing ever fazed him. I placed my hands on my knees and gasped for air as Pernell walked over to a duffle bag that was resting on a handmade wooden table. He took out a pair of black wraps. A poster of Iron Mike Tyson wearing his heavyweight belt with a raised fist was pinned next to a heavy bag. Pernell had at least thirty trophies stacked on shelves, each trophy with a golden boxer nailed on top. There were first place medals evenly tacked to the wall above the trophies and pictures of him sparring wearing those silk shorts and a wife-beater. Stacks of old boxing magazines compiled on the floor next to a pair of Adidas boxing shoes that were tied together by the shoelaces. Seeing all of Pernell's accomplishments made me feel like I was in a boxing hall of fame.

"Look, young nigga," Pernell said as he made his way towards me, "you need to be ready to fight at all costs no matter the situation. Eses, rips, brosstown, babylons, all them niggas. Is you ready?"

"Ready for what?" I had a look of confusion on my face. We just fought a pack of eses and managed to escape from the fight scene. Wasn't that enough for the day? Before I could ask another question, Pernell's hand slapped me across the side of my head.

"Always be ready." I glared at him in shock but before I could do anything, he slapped me again.

"Come on, blood. Put your fucking hands up." Pernell flinched, and I finally reacted. "It's about time, nigga." He grabbed my hands and began wrapping each one tight. I didn't know why I was so scared. I guess it was an emotion I was used to feeling. I didn't want to ask Pernell what he was doing because that would show signs of fear, and I wasn't no buster. So I told myself.

"How does that feel?" Pernell asked once he was done wrapping my hands.

"It feels fine," I spread my fingers moving them up and down before clutching them into a ball.

"Let me see your stance." I stood up straight and placed my fist in front of my face. I tried to remember the few bouts I'd seen on TV since that was the only formal education I had in boxing.

"Bend your knees, nigga." Pernell pushed me, and I took a few steps back. "If you stand like that in a fight, you take away your power and balance. Try to hit me."

"Huh?"

"You heard me, blood." Pernell slapped me a third time and his hands powered right through my fist, "You left an opening, and keep your chin down."

It didn't take much for me to catch on. I didn't want to get slapped repeatedly. With each slap to my head or cheek, I developed more anger, but no matter how angry I became, Pernell always kept his cool. I tried to catch him with a jab or hook, but he was light on his feet, dodging each one of my punches with his head movement.

"Get on your toes. You're too flat-footed."

I could see why Pernell had won all those trophies and medals. How come this kid wasn't training for the Olympics? I couldn't imagine anyone of Pernell's age beating him with his skill set. During our sparring session, he even put down his leading hand to give me more of an advantage. I didn't let up. I kept attacking Pernell, catching him a few times here and there. I didn't know if he let me hit him on purpose just to boost my confidence but my punches didn't faze him anyways. If I fought like him, I wouldn't be scared of anyone either.

Once we were done with our session, Pernell grabbed a few bottled waters that were in a mini-fridge. My mouth felt like cotton so I quickly gulped down the water. My shirt was drenched in sweat and I had developed a bloody nose. Pernell took some tissue that was already on the shelf and broke off a few pieces. He twisted the tissue and stuffed each one up my nostrils.

"I don't want to be all in your business, but where did you learn to fight like that?"

"My uncle." Pernell began unwrapping my hands.

"Is this his house?"

Pernell said nothing.

"Why did you stop?"

"I thought you weren't going to be all up in my business?"

"I was just wond-"

"Look, nigga," Pernell interrupted. He paused and stared dead into my eyes, "Just leave it at that. Be back tomorrow so you can work on hitting the mitts. Your footwork is sloppy as fuck, too. Take my jump rope, but bring that shit back," Pernell ordered. He walked back to the duffle bag and pulled out a properly coiled jump rope. He hesitated for a second, gripping the jump rope before tossing it my way.

"I didn't mean any disrespect." I wiped my forehead with my shirt and made my way out the garage door. The bleeding in my nose had slowed down, but I knew I would be sore in the morning. I had plans to go home and ice my shoulders. Who knows what Pernell would have scheduled for me tomorrow. I turned around before I made my way to the sidewalk, Pernell was holding one of the photos that was hanging by his medals. His face looked like it was made of stone and all of his boxing memories seemed to be in that single picture. I didn't say anything else to him, and I don't think he noticed me observing him.

On my way back home, I could only imagine the many hours Pernell put into just jump roping alone. The few times I ever tried to jump rope, I had whacked myself on my arm leaving whip marks. I noticed the jump rope was worn out in the middle and held together by duct tape. The smell reeked of old sweat that was collecting for years inside that duffle bag. On the handles was Pernell's name written with a Sharpie and next to his name was the word, Champ.

Chapter 6

—●◦●—

Over the next couple of weeks, I continued to hang out with Pernell and every day there was something new. This morning, I could hear Pernell's voice from the middle of the courtyard. "Wake your ol' I-love-my-pillow-ass up and come outside, nigga." I moved the blinds out of my way and opened the window. I saw Pernell posted by the stairs.

"Ight, let me throw some clothes on," I yelled through the window. Pernell was a morning person, waking up before everyone in the apartments. He was even up before Ms. Balboa, our complex manager, who collected rent bright and early on the first of every month. Even when kids are supposed to sleep in during these summer days, I could count on Pernell to knock on my window.

Stumbling to get my leg out of my sweats, my bedroom door crept open. My mom stood there wearing her favorite apron, a hand me down from her mother's mother. I could tell she was cooking my favorite breakfast because the smell of bacon followed her into the room and the dried yolk stain on the pocket of the apron was a dead give away. Her usual radiant smile was replaced with a frown, "Is everything ok, mom?" She didn't say a word but sat on the edge of my bed and patted the empty spot next to her.

"I can't sit right now, mom, Pernell is waiting for me outside."

"That's what I wanted to talk to you about," her voice trailed off, "you know I love you, right son?" Every time I heard those words, I knew it was something seriously bothering her. I thought about what I had done to get in trouble, and I hadn't been caught for anything yet.

I took a step closer to close the distance between us but I remained standing. "What's the matter then?"

Her tiny hand cupped my chin before she stood from my bed and went to look out my window. "Look son, your dad and I know how hard this move was for you, and we're happy that you found some new friends." *Here comes her famous 'but'.* "But I've noticed you've been coming in later than we agreed and your father said he's been detecting alcohol reeking from your bedroom at night."

It's the summertime. What did they expect? The sun is setting at eight o'clock, but I did admit, I had to

45

clean up my drinking. If Pops can still smell it on me after a twelve-hour shift, then I wasn't doing a great job of hiding it. Ever since Pernell showed me how to jack liquor from the nearby Ralphs, I've been drinking on a daily basis. Denying my mom's intuition would've kept me in that bedroom with her for another two hours, so I did what I knew best. I asked for forgiveness.

"I figured since it was summer, my curfew would be a little later." I wrapped my arms around her fluffy body and squeezed. I loved hugging my mom, it was like she was a gigantic teddy bear full of love. She squeezed back and rubbed her hands through my curly fro, like she used to do before she put me to bed after reading me a bedtime story.

"You can stay out an hour past sunset but nothing more. And if you violate that curfew, then kiss your Playstation and your outside privileges goodbye." Letting go of the reins was difficult for moms' to do since I'm the only child, but I'm glad she was starting to trust me. I jumped off the bed, kissed her on the cheek then hurried to throw on my 501's with my white Reebok Classics.

I opened the dresser drawer and grabbed the plastic bag I hid in there yesterday. I bought a fresh, white tee with the money I hustled from selling the liquor I jacked from Ralphs. The tee still had that slick crease down the middle.

"Where did you get that?"

In a rush to go outside, I forgot she was still here. "Um... Pernell gave it to me. He said his granny bought it for him, but it was too small. So, he gave it to me." Fuck, I didn't know what else to say and that was the first thing I came up with. It wasn't the best story, but it was something.

Her eyebrows raised halfway up her forehead. "Is that right?" I batted my eyes like I did when I was a kid, but that didn't seem to work anymore, "I was born at night but not last night. And by the way, we never talked about you and this drinking thing."

She caught me off guard with that statement, but I had to react fast. "It was probably the mouthwash he was smelling." Another bullshit on the spot story. I threw my shirt over my head, praying she would buy that lame-ass excuse.

"Quit trying to play me, boy," I erased my smile before I put my head through the hole of my shirt, "you ain't too old for me to put your father's belt to that skinny ass."

Moms' was right. I wasn't too old for an ass-whooping, and she made sure to remind me of that every year.

"It won't happen anymore." Stuffing my house keys in my front pocket I headed for the door, but she blocked my exit.

"I've been talking to some of the parents in the apartments, and they've been telling me that Pernell is somewhat of a…"

"Bad influence," I finished her sentence, "don't listen to that mess. They hating."

My mom's petite hands quickly slapped me across the face. Those small hands felt like they belonged to a heavyweight boxing champ. "Shut the fuck up. You sound stupid right now. Ain't no parent gonna be hating on no little ass boy," she slapped me again to make sure her point was understood loud and clear, "all I'm saying is you need to be careful. Not everyone has your best interest at heart."

I looked up at my mom and she stared back at me without blinking an eye, which made me know for sure she wasn't playing. "Yes, ma'am," I quivered, rubbing the pain from my cheek as I managed to get out the words she wanted to hear.

Chapter 7

My Mom's petite hand packed a heavy sting across my face. It felt like I was sparring all over again with Pernell. Walking out of the apartment, I made sure to lock the screen door behind me, I don't need another hand across my cheek later. Before turning around to head down the stairs, I tried to shake off my mom's suspicion about me and Pernell hanging out but the confidence she slapped out of me made it hard for me to do.

Pernell stood waiting at the bottom of the concrete stairs with his back turned towards me, his head slightly forward moving from left to right.

"What's good, my nigga? You wanna hit this?" he said as he turned my way. Pernell had that intuition that someone was close by even if he couldn't see them. It was like he never let his guard down. Pernell held a tightly rolled Swisher Sweet that he was running a flame underneath, drying the blunt. I took a quick glance over my shoulder to see if my mom was peeking out the blinds and sure enough, I spotted one singular blue eye spying through the middle of the blinds. I shook my head while Pernell laughed and pushed himself off the stairs in the direction of the security gate that encompassed our section of the apartments. "Come on scary ass nigga. Let's go."

I followed Pernell as we made our way to the street. He took a quick pause standing on Alta View Drive, the morning sun bouncing off his freshly brushed waves. His chest was poked out a little more than usual, and his chin raised higher this morning. He grabbed the blunt from behind his ear and set it between his lips while he grappled for his lighter in his pocket.

"You remember baby girl I told you about that stay across the street from Ralphs?" I nodded, remembering a story on how he took her virginity a couple of months back. "Well, her parents left last night for a month. She said she wanted me to slide through, and she told me that her best friend was there." I cocked an eyebrow because I had a feeling I knew the friend he was talking about. Baby girl's name was Krystal. I've only seen her once, and it was from a distance when Pernell was spitting his game. Even from afar, Krystal was thick in all the right places, her black jeans wrapped around her round ass, her titties waiting to bust out her red tank top, and her three-inch high heels made her legs even more luscious. Plus, it didn't hurt that she had the facial structure of Halle Berry. If Krystal's homegirl was half as beautiful as her, then I was already winning. I kept my excitement bottled up inside because I didn't want Pernell to see how eager I was to get over there.

Pernell stepped off the curb and what seemed like only a few strides was already on the other side of the street. Pernell and I were about the same height, but his strides were like that of someone who stood seven feet tall. I had to jog to keep up with him. In between breaths, I finally committed myself to ask Pernell a question I've been curious to know the answer to for the last month now.

"Aye Y.A.," Pernell's strides became shorter as he slowed down looking back at me. As I reached him, he had a Kool-Aid smile plastered across his face. It must've been that I finally remembered not to use his government name or maybe he was excited about meeting up with Krystal and her homegirl, too. "Why do you always cross the street and walk against traffic?"

Pernell's smile quickly evaporated, and he drilled his index finger directly into my sternum. "Rule number one, nigga. Never get caught slippin from behind. Always see what's coming at chu."

"I get it. Y.A. It was just something I noticed the last few times we were out. So what's up with them females?" I quickly changed the subject.

We continued our path and Pernell filled me in on Krystal's homegirl. This only excited me even more, and I did my best not to smile. I kept imagining her ass up in the air as I grabbed her hips, sliding inside her. I ran that image in my mind over and over until it was interrupted by what sounded like a gorilla trying to beat its way out of someone's trunk. An apple green 1988 Super Sport Monte Carlo on 18-inch gold daytons pulled up to our side. Even though the window was rolled halfway down, the limousine tint made it hard to see the driver's face. All I could see was a Boston Celtic cap bobbing to the beat that was escaping his trunk.

Pernell's jaw tightened as he threw his hands in the air, "What's hatnin, nigga?" The driver lowered his music and rolled his window all the way down. The smile that stretched across his face resembled the one I saw on Pernell's face a few seconds earlier.

"What's brackin', nigga?" the driver yelled back.

"You know what's brackin', nigga. I don't give a fuck who your pops is. Ain't no mo passes, ru! You need to quit sliding through the set, nigga!" Pernell stepped closer to the curb.

The driver laughed at Pernell's threats and readjusted his cap towards the back. Now, I was able to get a clear view of his face. His rich black skin and short french braids hanging underneath his cap were the only things that differed from Pernell's, but everything else looked identical, from the marble shaped eyes to the way the corner of his mouth curled like the Joker when he smiled. He leaned the top half of his torso out the window, his black Nike gloves slapped the outside of his door.

"Fuck you, you bitch ass nigga. I go where the fuck I want. On the Blood gang, B!"

Pernell didn't say another word. He was done talking. He launched himself off the curb and sprinted in the direction of the Monte Carlo. Pernell quickly pulled out a chrome .45 from his waistline. This caught me off guard. Pernell never mentioned owning a gun in any of our conversations.

"Y.A. it ain't worth it," I interrupted slapping his arm, but he didn't seem to hear me. I did my best to convince Pernell out of a potential life sentence, but there was no talking him out of it. His eyes were red,

BANGIN' *The Making Of A Y.G.*

and his breath grew heavier with each pulse. Pernell aimed the .45 directly at the driver's forehead. The driver's eyes stared back at Pernell like he didn't give a fuck if he got shot. Neither of them flinched. We all stood still, and we waited as Pernell cocked his finger back over the trigger to fire.

B Braze

Chapter 8

Staring down the barrel of a muthafuckin' Ruger wasn't new to me. It's been like this fo' the last five summers and when you're active and brackin' it comes with the territory. What is new, is staring down the barrel of a pistol my gay ass pops gave my bitch ass relative. I shouldn't expect anything less, especially since I'm the one doing all the clackin' out here.

The cloth I'm cut from is different than most of these niggas in the Southeast, most of these busters be hollywooding out here but I'm really about that shit. Broad daylight, at the mall, in front of niggas kids, or at cha mammy house, I just don't give a fuck.

That's how I knew my bitch ass relative Pernell wasn't finna pull the trigger, he still had too much life still dancing around in his little beady ass eyes. Once you're responsible for putting your enemies' homies face on their shirts you ain't gonna let no skinny ass buster next to you tell you "it ain't worth it," we out here bangin' everything is worth it!

Pernell has been a buster since the days he used to get dropped off at our granny's house on Willie James Jones and Ocean View Blvd, down in the cul-de-sac. It didn't matter if Pernell did anything to me or not, I would chastise him because I knew one day he'd be from the other side so I made it a habit to cup-slap the shit out of him every time he walked his happy ass by me. On summer days I couldn't wait for granny to give us some change for the ice cream truck, I would snatch his pockets right off his cheap ass jeans and take everything she gave him.

On Pernell's 7th birthday granny went all out and pieced together a full-fledged Batman-themed party for the nigga when the most she's ever done for me was take me to the run down Chuck E Cheese behind Price Breakers where half the machines never worked. She even put streamers and balloons in the front yard with a supersized fuckin' jumper in the back to match. On top of that, to make matters worse, my pops, the muthafucka I only see twice a year, was out in front of the house at the ice cream truck buying Pernell a batman shaped ice cream to match the fuckin' mask he brought him earlier.

If I ever imagined to have any superpowers in my life then that was the day. I tried as hard as humanly possible to burn a fuckin' hole through the back of his chest with my eyes. It must've worked because his bitch ass turned my way and smiled, then slid a ten-dollar bill out from the wad of money he had wrapped with a rubber band and stuffed it in Pernell's batman utility belt. Then his bitch ass gave me a head nod like I was his homie and hopped in his Impala and smashed off.

There was no way on God's green earth I was finna let Pernell enjoy that muthafuckin' ice cream. Before my pops made the right on Willie James Jones, I bee-lined straight towards Pernell's bitch ass who was sitting on the edge of the green box next to the Mexican twins about to take his first bite. Before he put his big crusty lips over the bubble gum eyes I slapped the ice cream so far out his fuckin' hand that it landed on the trunk of granny's Buick LeSabre parked in the driveway.

I pressed my forehead against the batman mask he was wearing. "I better not ever see you at granny house again. I don't give a fuck what day it is." I noticed his teary eyes behind the gay ass mask he was wearing so I pressed my forehead even harder. "And if you go tell on me like you normally do, this might be the last birthday you ever gonna see!"

The annoying chirping sound from my phone brought me back to reality. The name on the caller i.d. made me forget about Pernell's bitch ass immediately. I've been waiting on this bitch Sky to hit me back for the last three weeks. I pressed talk, hit the speakerphone, and threw my phone on the bucket seat next to me, "Sky, what's brackin'? It's been a minute. Tell me something good, ma."

Sky's the little rip bitch I've been fuckin' with for the last handful of months. When I was in the bounty jail I got a kite that Lil Blue Rocc smoked my older relative the day after St. Patrick's Day. I knew I had to get my get back as soon as possible and little did Sky know she was finna be the one to help me get it. Word had it that Sky fucked with any nigga whose name was ringin in Southeast, it didn't matter where he was from, she was fuckin' with him. So I knew I had her.

The thing about Sky was she lived with her aunty who stayed smack dead in the middle of the rip niggas turf, right on the corner of 41st and F, directly across from the church. Even though I hated rip pussy she was one of the baddest bitches in the Southeast, way badder than the thick chocolate Moniece bitch that stayed in the apartments behind Fam Bam and she was killin' Puerto Rican Amanda that lived on the corner of 61st and Alderley.

"So what's up? You got some info fo'a nigga or what?" I asked looking into my rearview mirror making sure I wasn't being followed.

"You know I do, daddy."

By the time Sky was done spilling the beans, I was five blocks away. Pulling up to the red light on 43rd something in my peripheral caught my eye. In the middle of a group of pisas waiting on their fish tacos at the Mariscos truck there were two niggas blued the fuck up. Their clothes were so goddamn bright it felt like that ugly ass color was burning a hole in my fuckin' retinas. The shorter of the two I didn't recognize but the high yellow one, the one who had his rag hanging down to the bottom of his muthafuckin' chucks, that nigga right there, that was the nigga I was looking for. That's that bitch nigga Lil Blue Rocc.

I could spot that high yellow Big Bird looking muthafucka from a mile away. We've been funkin' since the days I played Pop Warner at Valencia Park, and he played for Balboa. It was right after we beat them niggas in the Q Bowl 42-24 that me and the homies beat the brakes off the nigga. He was at the concession stand in front of the line running off at the mouth to the chick behind the register. "Cut it out, baby. Them slob niggas only won cuz' we wasn't at a hunnid percent out there. If we had our..." Before he got another word out of his disrespectful ass mouth I pushed my way to the front of the line where me and five other homies green-lighted the dog shit out of his high yellow ass and I ran my cleats all across his face.

Now amongst all the looky-loos in the parking lot, Lil Blue Rocc still didn't notice me at the red light. His dumbass was so concerned about his food he kept his eyes on the styrofoam plate being handed to him out the window. I rolled my passenger window down and reached between my seat and the middle console and grabbed the Desert Eagle then aimed right at the crooked line in the back of his head that split his french braids in two. If the ranchero man with the cowboy hat and ostrich boots would move two feet I could have had me another K for the set.

I sat there waiting for five seconds but the muthafucka didn't move and the fuckin' light finally turned green. I stuffed my Eagle back in its spot and slammed my left foot on the brake and my right foot on the gas at the same damn time. Me smoking my tires finally got them niggas attention and both of them spun their heads around like the bitch from the Exorcist.

The young nigga froze up like a deer in headlights but Lil Blue Rocc did exactly what I expected him to do. He turned around, pistol drawn, and I bee'd the scar from my cleat slashed across his yellow face from years earlier. I knew he wanted to pull the trigger but I knew he wouldn't, there were just too many witnesses. "What's brackin' nigga?!" I was loud enough so that everyone within fifty yards could hear me but before I played with his bitch ass any longer and miss my opportunity, I hit the gas and tossed a fat B out the window.

After I banged the right on Raven, halfway down I put my Monte Carlo into neutral and coasted the remaining fifty feet to F Street. By the time it came to a complete stop I was ready to hop out. I was right on the corner of Raven and F but I had to hurry down the alley so I could beat Lil Blue Rocc's bitch ass to Sky's aunty's house.

Underneath the cigarette lighter I pushed a button that I had Hector from down the street install for me when it was triv a couple years back. In seconds my little secret banthin opened up on the floorboard behind my driver seat. A door the length of a baseball bat slid open, I snatched my ridah's out my back pocket then the black hoodie in the backseat and tossed them on before I picked up my muthafuckin' baby. She was the bitch I trusted with my life and after three k's with her why wouldn't I? My pistol grip mossy never let me down.

Before steppin' out I stuffed her down the right side of my jeans and pulled my hoodie as far as I fuckin' could over my hat. Didn't need to draw any more attention to myself or my face. I was already known to every enemigo around here plus I didn't need any nosey ass neighbors catching a glimpse of me and snitching.

Crossing the alley I bee'd the beat-up Chevy Suburban sitting on 41st and F just like Sky told me. That was my spot and I had to get there before them niggas did so I ducked walked my ass to the back of the Suburban so that no one could bee me through the aquarium size windows in the front. With my back against the double doors I waited for the first voice I heard.

Tiny Blue Rocc

Chapter 9

— • —

It doesn't matter what I try to buy. Every time I'm at the counter, old man Oscar always asks to see my Id. Maybe it was from all the notes I passed him over the years from my grandpa OK-ing him to sell me a pack of cigarettes that gave my age away but none of that should matter today. Today's a celebration and old man Oscar shouldn't be asking me shit. Today, they dropped the murder charges on my cig homie for the crosstown that he smoked the day after St. Patrick's Day.

Lil Blue Rocc and I've been homies since our group home days up in the mountains ten years ago. He was the first and only person I listened to after they took my older brother from me and shipped him somewhere up North. We acted like brothers because we were brothers.

At Juvenile Hall he and I were celly's in unit 1000 for three months before they shipped him off to YTS. I wrote all his letters to his girl because he told me I knew how to strike hella good. Today is the first day I'm kickin' it with him since he got out of YTS . Not that I cared much that we kept missing each other on these streets but it damn sure feels good when we are able to link up and get it in.

I turned the back corner of the chip aisle and grabbed the little black box hanging next to the Extenze pills leading up to the counter. I can't believe Oscar's following my every move like I'm little Jose from around the corner who licks his ass every other day for at least a 12-pack of Natural Ice. I pointed to the grape swishers hiding behind his walrus sized belly, "Oscar quit playin' and move that belly of yours and put four packs of Swishers on the counter."

From behind I felt Lil Blue Rocc approaching and when he got to my left I could still feel the chill from the freezer sticking to his shirt. He slid the two cans of 211's on the counter and tossed a dub at Oscar's fat ass stomach. "Ring up everything you see on this counter and give cuz my change."

Oscar hated being told what to do but he knew the drill. He knew Lil Blue Rocc wasn't one to play with and he shouldn't start today, especially today. Oscar took all the items off the counter and tried stuffing everything into one paper bag and pushed it to me. "Now, Oscar, if you don't quit playing and put this shit in separate bags. You know you don't want the homie to have to come bacc in here and get on that ass."

When I got outside to the parking lot Lil Blue Rocc was in the middle of a crowd of Mexicans shoving his way to the front of the line at the Mariscos Truck. I should've known that was where he was going to be, every nigga I know has to get some Mexican food when they get out, no matter how long they've been locked up for.

Finally at the front of the line, Lil Blue Rocc nodded for me to come to him. It was easy for him to push through the crowd when he's 6'5 and built like Tim Duncan but for me it's another story when you're 5'6 and no bigger than the person next to you. Getting to the front I damn near had to fight about three pisas. Each pisas I pushed passed looked at me like I had lost my rabbit ass mind.

By the time I made it to the front of the line Lil Blue Rocc grabbed the rectangular styrofoam plate out the window and stretched his arm my way. I can hear my grandpa's voice now, telling me how I shouldn't be eating food from these nasty ass trucks but he isn't here right now and I'm hungry as fuck. All I've eaten today was some Saliditos and we all know you can't eat too many of them before you pass out from high blood pressure.

Before I was able to grab the styrofoam plate from Lil Blue Rocc's hand it fell on the lady in front me who was breastfeeding her daughter. Her screaming and yelling was loud as fuck but it wasn't because I dropped a plate of rolled tacos on her it was because Lil Blue Rocc was standing next to her with a Glock 40 in his hand aiming it over her head at a green Monte Carlo smoking its tires at the dead light.

Out of habit I patted my hip and I forgot I was naked. I let Baby Hoodie hold it last night so he could hit that lick with Tiny Awol. I'm sicc as fucc watching Lil Blue Rocc aim his pistol at the slob nigga in the street cuz if I would've had mine on me I would've been busted on the nigga. I wouldn't have cared how many witnesses were around us, I hated all them niggas with a passion. Not one of them niggas get a pass from me but before Lil Blue Rocc could pull the trigger the Monte Carlo peeled off. "I told you them faggot ass niggas is scarry, cuz." He was right, all them niggas is bitches. They only act tough when they're around their homies. I ain't never seen a slob nigga stand up on his own when he's by himself.

Jonas Royster

Lil Blue Rocc tapped my shoulder. "Let's hurry up, cuz, and get the fucc up outta here and get to that bitch house. Where you say she stay again?"

"She stay right there in the baby blue house next to old crazy Willie on 41st."

69

Chapter 10

"What's brackin' now, bitch-ass niggas?"

Forty feet in front of us is the same nigga that was at the dead light ten minutes ago, now he was holding a chrome Mossberg at our face. My stomach hit the sidewalk faster than the 211 out of my hand and when I looked at Lil Blue Rocc to gauge his reaction I heard a low growl behind me. "Aye, crab ass nigga, all eyes on me." Right as I turned my head to face my fate Lil Blue Rocc caught the first slug in his chest, right below his shoulder. I tried grabbing him so he wouldn't fall but another explosion came right after that. This time Lil Blue Rocc's eyes closed as the slug ripped through his stomach and exited out his back.

Lying next to Lil Blue Rocc in the gutter was his Glock 40 and I needed to get to it so I could get this nigga up off of us. The puddle of blood forming underneath Lil Blue Rocc's body was starting to run over the curb and my only hope was to leap over his body, grab the Glock, and roll behind the buggy and start busting. As soon as my hand gripped the Glock my finger didn't stop squeezing until the shells quit tap dancing on the sidewalk then it got real quiet. Then the next thing I heard was some tires peeling off in the alley.

When I looked down at the homie lying on the curb there was no life left in him. I mean all the gangsta that was there moments ago was gone. Wasn't shit else I could do but take his rag out his pocket and lay it under his head. "I know I fucc'ed cuz up but on gawd, I'ma make this right. On the hood."

Deshaun

Chapter 11

Day 28:

My new friends are nothing like Alex and Lee. Everyone on this side of town walks to their own beat like society's rules don't apply to them, maybe because they don't, but I have to admit this summer has been far more exciting than the ones I would spend hours in the library with Lee completing our extra credit projects for the summer.

Half the stuff I'm doing now with Pernell is borderline illegal but no one is really getting hurt other than a Russian security guard at Ralphs and a handful of *eses* at the trolley stop. But the stunt Pernell pulled a week ago at the light on the way to Krystal's; pulling out a pistol in broad daylight at his relative, was starting to push the envelope. Maybe if Pernell would've told me he had a pistol on him I might have declined walking with him but then again, I probably would've kept my mouth shut and went along anyway.

To be honest, I don't know what I would've done if he told me he had a pistol, but what I can say, that blitz of adrenaline that surged through my limbs from seeing Pernell standing on the corner pistol drawn, was like that same nervous energy I felt on the football field underneath the bright stadium lights on Friday nights.

If it wasn't for me seeing the hood of the police car creeping around the corner of the Jack In The Box, I wonder how far Pernell would've taken it. I guess the real question I should be asking myself is how far am I willing to take it? Out here, the only two people that get respect are the ones in front of the gun or the ones behind the trigger but sooner or later I'm going to have to choose which one of those I want to be.

Chapter 12

———•◦•———

The pounding on my bedroom door prompted me to toss my journal as far as I could underneath my bed. Standing there with a hand on her hip, cordless phone in the other, my mom's plump body filled my doorway, "Here, it's for you." She fired the phone at my chest before I could stand up. "Deshaun, tell your disrespectful ass friends don't be calling my house using no damn nicknames. His momma didn't name him no damn 'Slim'!"

Hearing from Slim was a surprise, other than smoking a couple blunts with him and Pernell we've never talked much. Slim's falsetto pitch was compressed through the phone line, he didn't take a single breath as he relayed the message he was told to give to me. The only thing I heard was "Pernell said to meet him at the park at noon and don't be late," then there was a click.

Pernell skipping to knock on my window as he passed by this morning didn't make any sense, this has been our routine since I've been hanging out with him. The uneasiness swimming around in my stomach almost had the Frosted Flakes from earlier climb their way out of my mouth and onto the floor, next to the Chargers clock that fell when my mom slammed the bedroom door. I took the 501's I had laying between my bed and box spring and slid them on and tossed on a red shirt I got from the liquor store earlier that week.

Looking at myself in the mirror I notice I'm not the same kid I was a couple of months ago. My curly afro is now freshly braided, I've donated my school uniform Dockers to Goodwill for a pair of Levi's, even the way I'm speaking is changing by the minute. I glance at the mirror one last time before I run my hand down the crease of my jeans, tie my Reebok Classics, and head to the front door for the park.

Walking down AltaView to the park, I kept my head on a swivel and made sure to walk against the flow of traffic, not wanting a repeat of what happened yesterday especially since I don't have any protection like Pernell had. If there was one thing I learned yesterday, it was that everything matters out here, and not following the rules and laws of the street is a matter of life or death.

I crossed through the parking lot of Ralphs backtracking my steps the day I followed Pernell to the park a couple weeks back. The stairs between the

Ralphs and the Taekwondo studio looked like they led to heaven; they were so tall. They were only three hundred yards away from the bottom of the hill that leads to the park. The Ponderosa pines sprinkled along the street shade me from the summer sun that keeps trying to tattoo the African Pride greased between my braids.

At the bottom of the hill, the aroma from the smokers crept their way into my nostrils practically made me tipsy. The alchemy between the smoke and the slow burning ribs could've made anyone intoxicated if they stood there long enough.

Coming over the crest of the hill I've never seen so many red bandanas in my life, it didn't matter if they were in their sixties or in strollers, walking or rolling in a wheelchair, everyone had a red bandana hanging off of them. One chick got so creative; she had her twin daughters in red bandana diapers with matching knockers in their hair.

Fifty yards in front of me underneath a steel gazebo next to two cement tables, Pernell was kneeling on the sidewalk bouncing a pair of red dice across the cement. The half-moon of people standing around kept dropping money to the ground while

Pernell's hand was like a dealer's rake sweeping it all in.

"Aye, ru, who da fuck is you?" Turning to my blind side there was a guy hovering over me, his Franklin batting gloves covering up his fist. His face I didn't recognize behind his purple black skin.

"Deshaun," I answered.

"I don't know no muthafuckin' Deshaun, nigga!"

"Pernell told me to meet him up here." Pernell's government name slipping out of my mouth made my soul cringe. This isn't the time for me to forget any rules. "I mean Y.A., he said for me to meet him up here at noon."

His eyes narrowing with skepticism, his next words confirmed my mistake. "Who the fuck is you, nigga, the feds?!" He took a step away from me like I was wearing a wire and pulled his sagging jeans above his hips. "You gots to P up, ru!"

One thing being around Pernell has shown me is never back down no matter what the situation is. He said in the streets, you have to guard your reputation with your life or else someone will take it. "I ain't finna go nowhere, you got me fucked up." I took a step closer acting braver than I felt.

Before I put my hands up he slipped a jab aimed at my face, then a wild right hook swung over my head. The training from the garage was kicking in. Bouncing on the balls of my feet I took a step back to measure him up and squared off. Before he said another word, I used my back foot to launch myself forward and connect with a short hook to his chin. It stopped him from advancing but it didn't park him.

He shimmied his jaw then spit a loogie of blood. "On Piru, I'm finna work the dog shit out you."

"Kill the body and the head will die", were always Pernell's instructions. Six inches from his chest I start beating his body like an old pillow that needs fluffing. The blood from my broken skin is starting to leave skinny trails of blood across his white shirt, his boney ribs smashing against my knuckles felt like I was hitting a brick wall, but with every punch, he's starting to shrink to my size.

He extends his arms to gain distance, but I move in closer. Pivoting my back foot I explode through his ribs with a right hook, his back leg buckles and his knee hits the grass. Sliding to my left, I'm in the perfect position to finish him off but the tremors rolling under the balls of my feet made me look to my right. The wave of red coming my way made it impossible for me to take another breath, my lungs were suspended in time and my legs wouldn't budge.

From the mass of people, Pernell's voice bellied over the wave. "Boguard, bick it." Boguard placed his hand on his knee and pushed himself up. "Blood's with me." Pernell stepped into the circle and in between us. "Is there a problem with that?"

Walking to the other side of the park was hard to do, people were shoulder to shoulder drinking and smoking, not paying me any mind but as soon as they saw Pernell it was like they saw a celebrity and gave him the red carpet. Pernell knew everyone out there, from the OG's to the babies in the strollers. It seemed like there wasn't a girl he didn't hug and a guy's hand he didn't shake. Pernell tugged on the sleeve of my shirt. "Come on. We finna smash to the tables. I want you to meet some of the big homies."

Pernell pointed towards an older dude on the bench playing dominoes. His Shirley Temples were as silky as a spider's web, the only thing that revealed his age was the light dashes of gray sprinkled throughout. Years of smoking put his voice in a headlock, his growl made him sound like he was talking under water. "What's brackin', little nigga?"

I kept my mouth shut and nodded. His eyes never left mine. He was searching for something but I didn't know what. His eyes had their own story, one of an old general, one who'd seen countless wars and endless deaths but too addicted to throw in his rag. Standing up from the table he towered over everyone in our radius. His physique was in immaculate shape.

I extended my hand and reached over the table, his massive paw formed the sixteenth letter in the alphabet. Following his lead I did the same thing and our three fingers interlocked over the table. The strength in his grip brought a numbness in my hand, but I didn't release.

"This right here, little nigga." He squeezed tighter. "This P represents everything you p around you right now. This oath is like no other. Not one muthafucka here is bigger than this PIRU!" He released my fingers and took a swig from his red, plastic cup. "And for the record, little nigga, I'm O.G. P-Nutt."

Arm & Hammer pushed his way through the crowd of people around us and was within inches of Pernell's face. "What the fuck is blood doing up here?"

Arm & Hammer stuck his finger in my face. "Ain't no one told his square-ass to bome up here!"

Pernell moved an inch closer eliminating any space they had left. "I told blood to bome up here, I'm vouching for this, nigga."

Arm & Hammer's eyes grew as wide as silver dollars. "You know what today is, nigga!" Pernell continued to smile. "It's muthafuckin' set day, you know we don't bring no squares to the park."

To the right of P-Nutt was a man no taller than five feet, his squid ink skin glistened from the sweat pouring off his bald head. The burn mark along his cheek reminded me of a Senegalese warrior I saw with my dad when we visited Senegal on a summer vacation a couple of years back. "Both of you niggas need to shut the fuck up! This is how we gon' settle this." He pushed past Arm & Hammer and slapped his hand on my chest. "Is you ready to bang, little nigga?"

Chapter 13

T he longer I waited, the more difficult my breathing was becoming. I shifted my short breaths from my chest to my nose so no one would notice my fear. I'm in the lion's den and there's no backing out now. Pernell and Arm & Hammer are the first two in front of me. From the corner of my eye, Fly was 45 degrees to my right and Boguard was trying to sneak himself to my blind side. P-Nutt walked from behind the four and stepped onto the sidewalk. "A'ight, young hyenas, do what you do.."

Boguard darted at me, his giraffe strides put him within arm's reach in a matter of seconds but I was ready this time. I swung my fist like an ax. Bingo. Man down. His body melted into the grass in front of me. No time to admire my work, I jumped over his body and bolted to my next obstacle. Fly was shorter than me by a half of a foot but that didn't hinder his ability to pack a hell of a punch. My rib bent to his knuckles when he connected with a short hook, but I kept moving forward, kept swinging. I'd miss some, but then I swung more.

Then I felt it, from my jaw to my lumbar region. I laid flat in the grass, a waterfall of electrical streaks flashed in front of my eyes blocking the sun. The pain in the joint of my jaw next to my ear had my jaw locked shut. Arm & Hammer towered over me, his arms raised in the air. "I knew you weren't ready, nigga!"

Pushing myself off the grass the only person I saw was Pernell. He was eight feet in front of me, smirking, pulling his gloves tighter around his knuckles. The emptiness in his eyes is the same as I saw the day at the trolley, he was emotionless. Watching him walk towards me I felt like a gazelle in the Serengeti. I put my guard up just as we practiced in the garage but that didn't help much. My head was turning into a speed bag and he relished every second of it. The more I moved my forearms to block where I thought he was punching next, he would hit me in the spot I just left open. I moved my guard up to block my chin and he connected with a punch so fucking hard to my ribs I folded like a lawn chair.

It took every ounce of strength to push myself onto my knees and hands but that's as far I got, I couldn't move any further. My thoughts were telling me to get up but my body wasn't responding. Pernell's voice caught me off guard, his outstretched hand pulled me to my feet. I stretched my jaw to make sure nothing required me to go to the hospital. "You did alright, nigga. Next time keep ya hands up and roll off the punches as I taught you."

Walking with Pernell to the tables felt different this time. I am now a part of them, the family, a circle of loyalty I wouldn't break. The looks of uncertainty were replaced with eyes of admiration and respect. The same guys that ran up on me, ready to kick my ass when I was fighting Boguard were now the same ones shooting me the P and handing me blunts to smoke and Hennessy to drink.

From the crowd, a hand gripped my shoulder and stopped me in my tracks. When I spun around his right hand was already shaped in the letter of a P. He was shorter than P-Nutt and looked ten years younger but that didn't take away from his stature. His margarine complexion made him stand out amongst everyone else. The scar that ran from the corner of his ear lobe to the crease of his mouth made his face show its age. I copied my hand to match his and our three fingers interlocked together.

"I'm Double O.G. Red." I tried not to take my eyes away from his stare. "Do you know what today is, little nigga?" I didn't say a word. "Today is set day."

He released my hand and tossed his P, high in the air. "Today is the day we show love to the homies that lost their lives for the set and to the homies that are in the stoops behind this P funk." As Red talked, everyone around us stopped their chattering and showed him respect. "Check this out, young nigga. Ain't no one around here bigger than this P. If a nigga ain't dead or in the pen and he ain't here today, then he ain't from the set. Bottom line. Today is about Piru'n, put-ons, and politicking; so, today is your lucky day, little nigga."

P-Nutt agreed with his ace. "Now, listen up. All you niggas need to hear this shit." P-Nutt hopped on the cement table. "What you niggas do reflect on the whole set, so watch your every move. If it doesn't fall under the five p's, then don't move."

I tapped Fly on his shoulder. "What's the Five P's?"

P-Nutt must've heard my question because he answered loud enough for everyone to hear. "Proper preparation prevents poor performance."

I repeated it to myself.

Red picked up where P-Nutt left off. "And bad association prevents it from being enormous."

I could tell these two had been lacing niggas like me for years. "Live it, breathe it, tattoo it, I don't give a fuck how, but nigga, embody this law and you'll be around for a long time. I'm 51 still brackin' and breathin'."

P-Nutt cleared his throat and found my eyes in the crowd. "Law two; and this one is more important than the first one, so listen up, nigga. Never snitch!" His eyes never blinked. "I don't give a fuck if the brosstown murk your momma, yo' sister, yo' little daughter... I don't give a fuck! We settle everything up under these streetlights and we don't say a muthafuckin' thing to the Babylons."

There was so much information being given I tried to comprehend everything thrown my way. Most of the stuff I've heard Pernell repeat before but the seriousness which Red and P-Nutt explained made it stick to my soul.

P-Nutt jumped off the tabletop with the grace of a cat and approached Pernell. "Whatchu finna do, little homie?" Pernell shrugged his shoulders and blew out a cloud of smoke. "I need you to shoot to the liquor store and grab some more blunts."

B Braze

Chapter 14

━━━◆◆◆━━━

Word on the street was, niggas had my name in their mouth like candy, it's been seven days since I smoked the crab nigga Lil Blue Rocc in front Sky's auntie pad and even though the homicide detectives ain't kicked in my momma door I knew I wasn't out the clear yet. Sky's voicemails kept me updated on what the detectives were doing while I was in Arizona. Every time Sky left her house she said she was being followed by the detectives. It didn't matter if it was to work, Oscars market around the corner, or to church, they kept someone on her bumper.

I would've stayed in Tucson with my baby momma longer but I had to come back for my sister's birthday. Darlene was turning 21 and just because the police were hotter than fish grease in the Southeast that didn't stop me from functioning with her especially because of all the times she's been there for me. I wouldn't miss this for a muthafuckin' thing in the world.

Darlene isn't my blood sister but my sister out of circumstance, I've known her longer than any of the homies from the set. Her momma and my momma were best friends and when they used to run around boostin' and hustlin' they thought it was best for both of them to move in with each other so we could watch ourselves while they did what they had to do to put food on the table. That was way back when me and Darlene were in the fourth grade and going to Knox Elementary together. The rest of our elementary years and a little into our junior high years we all lived together in the Bay Vista Apartments right next to the basketball courts.

I remember the nights we would sneak out our bedroom window when our mommas would be in the front hosting parties so that we could go bick it with the older homies in the trails. Even though Darlene rocked knockers in her hair and wore dresses back then she was a gangsta at heart. At thirteen years old she jacked some d-boy who was trying to fuck on her and gave me his deuce-deuce, that was my first pistol.

Now sitting on the white leather sofa at Darlene's own apartment watching her layout all the fits she jacked from Nordstroms for her 21st birthday soiree brought our lives full circle. The only thing fuckin' me up is the fact she is letting redhead Buster Rob fuck on her. Truth be told, I don't give two fucks who she fucks on, the only reason I introduced them was to keep him close for information.

Darlene threw on the jungle green Versace bodysuit that was neatly laid over the back of the dining room chair. "What cha'll think? Am I brackin' for tonight or what?" She spun around, put her hands on the wall in front of her, and made her ass roll like a wave of water. If I didn't respect the fact that she was like a sister to me, I would've ripped that bodysuit right off her chocolate skin and fucked her right in front of buster blood.

Buster Rob smacked Darlene on her ass and looked over at me for my reaction, his smile turned serious and he leaned in so I could hear what he had to say. "I just got word that your relative and his bitch ass homies are having a function in Paradise Hills at Zamorano park." Hearing that my faggot ass relative Pernell was there made me sit up and listen. "The little birdy said they're over there deep, we can go over there and knock one of them niggas off easily. I know exactly where that's at."

Buster Rob was right, my bitch ass relative and his gay ass homies were all finna be high, faded, and slipping. I can finally get my get back and this will be the perfect time to knock off Pernell for that gay ass hollywooding he pulled last week at the light, pulling a pistol on me and not using it. Grabbing my keys off the end table I tossed them on Buster Rob's lap."You ready nigga?"

Darlene walked her fine ass in between us and the giant TV pushed against the wall and motioned for me and Buster Rob to move. She must've been ear hustlin' because she slid the loveseat from the wall and handed me a black SKS and Buster Rob a chunky compact .45 caliber Ruger. "Ya'll niggas handle what needs to be handled but make sure your asses make it to the club tonight. Remember it's my birthday and I need my niggas there."

Chapter 15

———•••———

Waiting in a car for however long it's needed never bothered me. I've waited for twenty hours before scoping out a crab nigga who slapped my cousin in her mouth. For Pernell I'm willing to wait for muthafuckin' eternity if I have to. If I don't smoke another nigga in my life time this one will be worth it. We've been at the bottom of the hill at Zamorano park for what has felt like a fucking hour already. I wasn't really trippin' because the reward for smokin' Pernell's bitch ass was finna be the highlight of my muthafuckin' summer. If it wasn't for me being locked up for 240 days in Camp Barrett three summers ago, I would've been knocked off Pernell.

The plan was all lined up for the night of the Fourth of July. Me, Darlene, her homegirls, and gay ass Pernell were all at our granny house for her 70th birthday a week earlier. That was the day I decided that I was tired of looking at his bitch ass and I came up with a plan to sic one of Darlene's fine ass homegirls on Pernell so I could set him up and knock him off.

The plan was to have Darlene's friend set up a date with Pernell and take him to J Street pier to watch the fireworks and park in the back of the parking lot next to the bathrooms. Once the fireworks were to start she was going to excuse herself to the bathroom and that's when I would creep up from behind the car and wet that muthafucka up with a Mac 11 that I got from Darlene. If it wasn't for my probation officer doing a random fourth waiver search of my momma house the night before the mission and violating me for having an empty box of .380 bullets, Pernell's bitch ass would've been dead already.

Buster Rob was getting on my last fucking nerve as we waited for Pernell or one of his faggot ass homies to come down the hill. All he was motor mouthing about was how Pernell and his homies used to chastise him when he lived on this side of town. Now I understand why they called him a buster. There was nothing gangsta about him to save his life. If it wasn't for his uncle living next to my granny and him fucking with Darlene I wouldn't be bickin' it with his buster ass either.

Just as I was ready to smack the dog shit out of his buster blood, his arm shot across my face, and damn near knocked the blunt out my mouth. Buster Rob was pointing at the opening in between the bushes at the bottom of the hill and like magic, Pernell's gay ass was on a chrome Dyno that our granny bought him for his sixteenth birthday.

I turned the music down and slid as low as I could in my seat so that my head couldn't be seen from the outside. I kept my eyes on his every movement, his every pedal, the way he didn't look in our direction as we rode across the street. He was slipping and I was going to make him pay for his mistake. I leaned my seat as far as it would go back and laid the stock of the SKS across my chest.

I closed my eyes, I said a prayer for my granny then turned towards Buster Rob. He was ready, a green rag wrapped around the bottom half of his face, his eyes searching for my next command. I pointed at Pernell as he disappeared through the apartment complex. "Follow him but not too close, we're gonna catch his bitch ass as he comes down the stairs."

Tiny Blue Rocc

Chapter 16

I knew the cig homies were gonna hit me but not this fast, the rule was to always wait 47 hours before we congregated and got crackin' on some niggas, so getting this call and it has only been a day I knew something was different. The meeting was going to be at Lil Blue Rocc's momma house as soon as the sun dropped.

Ms. Jackson stayed on Escuela Street across from Gompers. She was the mom I hoped my mom would've become if my dad's brother wouldn't have shot her in the chest three times on Mother's Day and killed her. Ms. Jackson was a no-nonsense type of mom, she loved tough but fair.

The first time I ran into Ms. Jackson was almost my last time. I had just gotten back into Gompers after getting out of juvenile hall and I was only home two weeks this time before my cousin who went to Gompers with me, told me that Hector up the street, the one with all the cars in front of his house, was giving anyone who brought him a 380z five hundred bucks. My cousin knew my situation at grams house so any opportunity to get some money I was with it.

Later that week during lunch my cousin hit me up while I was eating a nasty ass ground beef minced meat pie they gave us for free, and told me he spotted a blue 380z on 14-inch gold Daytona's parked right across the street in front of a U-Haul on Escuela.

When the bell rang to go back to class we hopped the fence and ran across the street to the house with the Z. I stood at the trunk and my cousin on the other hand was by the driver's side door pulling out the Slim Jim. I must've been staring at my cousin too long because within a second there was a hard piece of steel pressing on the back of noggin. "Tell your stupid ass friend he better leave my fucking car alone or I'm finna blow that little ass brain of yours all over the roof."

Ms. Jackson didn't fuck around back then so now walking to her house felt crazy especially since I haven't talked to her since Lil Blue Rocc got smoked. Before I even got in the front yard the cries from the ladies inside were mixing with that Scarface and Pac song "Smile."

I kept my head down so I wouldn't be noticed and went to the gate on the side of the house like I was told to when I got the call. I peaked over the top to see where the homies were and to make sure Cocaine and Blue were chained up before I walked back there.

OG Blue Rocc and the rest of the older homies were at the end of the fence next to a plastic fold-out table with a giant picture of Lil Blue Rocc on top of it. About ten feet to the left of them were a group of about seven homies that were in Lil Blue Rocc's generation. The only two faces I recognized were Cowboy and C Style, the rest of them had their hoods over their heads and their hats pulled low.

I lifted the latch and pushed the gate open forgetting how narrow it was between the dog run and the side of the house. The first person that saw me walking in was Blue Rocc. He left the table and came straight to me. "Why the fucc is you walkin' up in here like ain't shit happened cuz?!" Blue Rocc grabbed two fist fulls of my shirt and lifted me off the grass and slammed my back against the stucco. "What the fucc happened that day, little ass nigga?"

Keeping my eyes focused on the one good eye the nigga had left I tried explaining what happened that day. The truth must've worked because he let my shirt go and started pacing back and forth. "So you tellin' me that you niggas saw cuz right before the shit happened?"

I didn't have shit to say I was stuck on stupid. My mouth was open but nothing came out. I fucced up and I knew it. I didn't follow any of the rules Lil Blue Rocc laced me on when I became his little homie. I didn't have a pistol on me, I let Nichelle know we were on our way too early and I didn't run a background check on who her cousin Sky was fucking with at the time.

I looked at Lil Blue Rocc's picture on the table and spoke up. "Yea we saw him at the light but I didn't think he was going to the same bitch house we were heading to."

C-Style came from around the corner of the house and stepped in between me and Blue Rocc. He tapped the barrel of his 9mm on my chest. "Why didn't one of you niggas dump cuz the fuck out when he was at the light?"

Since a nigga didn't want to get shot I politely pushed his barrel towards the ground. "Cause there were too many witnesses in the parking lot at the time."

Blue Rocc shoved C-Style out his way and was directly in my face, this time with both his hands wrapped around my neck. His hands were squeezing the air out of my lungs but I stood there and didn't budge, I took what I deserved. My eyes were losing focus but before a nigga passed out he let my neck go. "So what the fuck happened little nigga, speak?"

Ms. Jackson came storming around the side of the house and stared at the three of us. She didn't have to say a word if she didn't want to, her face said it all. She grabbed Blue Rocc by the sleeve of his shirt and pulled him away from my face. "Arthur, I'm tired of this shit. I invited y'all to my house so you can show your respect to my son, not for you old ass niggas to be bullying the young ones into going to kill someone." Blue Rocc didn't say shit to Ms. Jackson, he couldn't, she was right.

Ms. Jackson had four sons, her oldest, Crazy Sticc was the only one still alive. He was from the hood but I never met him, he's been in San Quentin on death row since 1984 for assassinating an undercover officer at Sundance gas station. Her two middle sons Garfield and Playdough died together in a shootout with some slob niggas at the 47th Street trolley station and now her youngest, my nigga, Lil Blue Rocc died in my arms.

The "I don't give a fuck attitude" I saw behind her eyes when she pulled her pistol on me years back was gone, her black mane was now filled with gray flakes and her heart was so heavy that it weighed down her gait. She pulled me away from the wall and drew me into her bosom and wrapped her arms around my frail frame. The sobs she let out next shook my soul, she wasn't only crying for Lil Blue Rocc, she was crying for each of her sons. I cradled her back wishing I could let out all my guilt and sorrow with her but I couldn't. I had to leave that pain trapped in me so I could unleash it out on my enemies.

Pulling away from Ms. Jackson's embrace I looked in her eyes. The bags underneath them dropped to her cheeks like she hasn't slept in days. I took a deep breath and said what I've been dreading to say since I fucked up and let Lil Blue Rocc get smoked. "I'm sorry Ms. Jackson. I'm sorry I wasn't able to prevent this from happening."

Ms. Jackson placed a finger over her lips for me to stop talking then placed her hands over her heart and bowed her head. "It's okay sweetie. I understand. God has him now." She raised her head and searched my soul with her eyes and placed her delicate hands on my shoulders. "Son, don't worry about it. He loved you like a brother. Just promise me you won't end up like him. None of this shit is worth it in the end."

Chapter 17

Rolling out of bed I couldn't help but stare at the 8 x11 flick on the wall above my dresser of Lil Blue Rocc staring right at me. It was the picture of me and him on family photo day at the group home eight years previous. We both were young as hell. I was no older than eight so that meant he had to be about twelve. Back in those days, I didn't give a fuck. If it wasn't for him looking out for me I prolly would've been on my way to T.S. or something. We weren't playing back in group home days, it was me and him against everyone else at that fuccin' place, staff included.

Last night, watching Ms. Jackson breakdown in front of me made it more real than ever on what I needed to do and how fast I needed to get it done. I need cuz momma who kill't the homie to feel the same way she did. Right before I cut last night Cowboy mentioned to me that his baby comma might know, cuz, who shot Lil Blue Rocc. She told him that the same green SuperSport we were looking for was always parked on La Paz every other Saturday, next to her slob ass cuzzin' house behind St. Rita's. Her cuzzin told her that the nigga name was some shit like B Braze.

Behind my headboard was a turkey bag filled with a half pound of chronic I was gonna give Lil Blue Rocc after we left the bitch pad but that never happened. I still don't know how that bitch ass nigga knew we were going there. The bitch Nichelle, which was Sky's cousin, wasn't even from Daygo so I know she ain't called him. She was visiting from Atlanta and had only been out here a month before me and the homies started running through her. Sky could have called cuz but why would she do some dumb shit like that. Her and Lil Blue Rocc used to be hella cool. It was just a couple of summers back her and cuz used to fuck around plus she lived in the hood her whole life. This shit was going to drive me crazy but I knew in time whoever set us up would come to light.

Before I made it to the bathroom the cordless phone next to the bed rang. It was Cowboy and I couldn't understand a word flying out of his mouth. Cuz only talked fast like this when something pressed his buttons. "What's craccin', cuz? Slow the fucc down."

"Them bitch ass yellow jackets just kicced in my d'owe, that's what's craccin' nigga" His words stopped me in my tracks and woke my ass up fast. "It was that wet dog smelling white boy Braveheart and his bitch ass 'Yes Men' from GSU that just fucced my shit up. They said they heard I was the one with Lil Blue Rocc that night the shit happened."

I knew how this scenario was going to play out because this wasn't the first time they kicked in me and my niggas doors. My granny house was always the next in line to get searched especially since Cowboy house was only the next street over. "When did the yellow jackets leave?" I asked looking over my room at all the shit I needed to hide in my granny's room.

"They left two minutes ago."

Detective Braveheart

Chapter 18

Eighteen years as a detective and these dumb mother fuckers still don't get it. There's nothing they can hide from me. I'm the mother fucker that runs these streets, not them. I have ears and eyes all over this son of a bitch. These cowards who they think are so super fucking gangster I've had on the payroll for years now.

I'm surprised Terrance or Tiny Blue Rocc, whatever he wants to call himself these days ain't tired of seeing this white face yet. The last time I was here I was able to book his ass on a ten-month violation for gang paraphernalia but that was only because I couldn't find the gun he used to rob the Burger King down the street. He and I both knew I was going to get his ass for something big.

Standing in this same spot I was a year ago I noticed they still hadn't fixed the frame from the time my boys and I visited last year. These people are so stupid and poor around here that they will go buy a new car before they buy a new door and secure their own safety. I took a step closer to the door and listened for the shuffling of feet, nothing. "Mrs. Williams you have three more seconds to open this fucking door. Three, two--."

The door swung wide open like I knew it would. Mrs. Williams' leathery face stood in front of me, her ashy hands hanging off her hip matched the dingy white robe she wrapped her sickly body in. "Now, Mrs. Williams you know the fucking routine," I pointed at the two rookies they gave me and gave them the go to move right past Mrs. Williams and head to the back of the house. "Your dumb ass grandson is a fourth waiver and this is a probation sweep so we don't need no damn search warrant or any other documents. When he waived his fourth amendment right, that gave us all the permission we need to come to your house any time we damn well please."

I placed my hands on both sides of Mrs. William's shoulders, moved her away from the door frame, and took my Oakley's off so she could stare the devil in his eyes. "Now, Mrs. Williams, I'm only going to warn you this one time and one time only. Don't get in our way or else I will have Greg over there cuff you up and have you arrested for obstruction. You got that?"

Being the lead detective meant that I didn't have to break a sweat tossing Terrance's room upside down but the rookies looked like they were enjoying every minute of it. They didn't waste any time ripping drawers out of the dresser and throwing every bit of clothing he owned all across the room. In the corner of the room by the closet in his boxers was Terrance, his hands cuffed behind his back face pressed against the drywall. There was something about seeing a nigger cuffed and powerless that made my good ol' American blood start to stir. "So, Mr. Tiny Blue Rocc, long time no see buddy."

These moments I live for. The power I have over these dancing monkeys makes my dick stand up in my pants. They think they are so tough but what I know from eighteen years of experience is that out of ten gang members that I press for information, six are going to tell me what I need to know and three will keep their mouths shut. But what really makes my days are the times I get the one hidden jewel, that one gangster who was faking being tough the whole time, the one who knew he couldn't do any jail time. Those are the ones I love flipping into my confidential informants.

The look on Terrance's face when he heard my voice was priceless. He knew why I was here and he knew I didn't want to hear any of his bullshit. I sat on the edge of his bed and patted for him to sit next to me. "Come join me, Terrance. We have a lot to talk about my friend." His voice was muffled by the drywall pressing against his mouth. "Terrance, now you know damn well why I'm here, so don't play stupid with me boy."

Gary let his forearm off the back of Terrance's head so could turn to face me. The slick ass smirk smudged across his face made me want to put a foot in his ass but I had something better than that. "Gary, do me a favor." Gary's bobbing head resembled the Trevor Hoffman bobblehead mounted on my desk. "Hogtie his dumb-ass."

Gary is my black goon who hated his skin as much as I did. For Christmas last year I bought him some bleaching cream and he hasn't stopped thanking me since. Gary lifted Terrance off his feet in one swift motion and slammed him on his chest next to me at the edge of the bed. "Hey dipshit, do you have anything else smart to say?" The blue bandana Gary stuffed in Terrance's mouth kept him quiet. "So now that I have your attention Tiny Blue Dick, who killed Lil Blue Rocc?" Terrance's eyes widened. "Word on the streets is you were the one next to him when he died."

Knowing how this fucker operated I figured he was going to keep his mouth shut but I wanted him to know I'm onto his black ass. There's nothing in the streets that I don't know about and to show Terrance never to call my bluff, I showed him the last five calls made to me within the last twenty-four hours. He kept his poker face nice and tight but his body tensed up when I showed him all the confidential informants calling me on an hourly basis. It's the way they tell on themselves without telling on themselves that always gives them away. Never fucking fails.

I took my prized butterfly knife I got from The Boys In Blue convention last year and cut the tie from around his ankles and sat his ass up on the edge of the bed so we can see eye to eye. "Listen up fuck face, today is your lucky day. I'm not going to book you on that little ass weed you think you're selling. Plus it's going to be hard to compete when your buddy Cowboy has the same trash ass weed up the street." Gary took the turkey bag filled with weed and dumped it all across the carpet. "I'm going to get you for the long haul, Terrance. I will have your ugly black face off these streets for good real soon."

Deshaun

Chapter 19

My adrenaline was fading and my body was starting to feel the effects of getting jumped in. I took a napkin off the table and dabbed above my eye. The blood wasn't leaking as it was a minute earlier, but I still kept it pressed against my eyebrow.

The sun was setting but it didn't look like anyone was leaving the park. Arm & Hammer and Boguard were still on their hands and knees shooting craps, Slim was behind me sitting on the other table smoking a blunt while Fly went to the cooler to grab him and me a tall can of Miller Genuine Draft.

Before I pushed the tab into the mouth of my can I heard what sounded like someone celebrating the Fourth of July early. It looked like no one else noticed but I knew I wasn't tripping. Then they went off again, this time it was a lot longer. I tapped Fly on his shoulder. "Did you hear that?"

Arm & Hammer lifted his head from the crap game and answered before Fly had a chance. "Hear what nigga? Only thing I hear is me breaking these niggas on the dice." Arm & Hammer stacked the dice on each other, shook them up then slid them across the sidewalk making them tap dance as they landed on the number he was calling out.

My focus was on Arm & Hammer picking up everyone's money that I didn't notice Pernell pedaling towards us. He looked three shades lighter and his eyes were the size of half dollars. In the couple of months of hanging with Pernell, I've never seen this look. He always came off as confident and in total control but right now as he rode up to the tables those two qualities had vanished.

Pernell jumped off the Dyno and let it ghost ride through the middle of the dice game. Arm & Hammer bounced to his feet and squared off. Pernell walked right on him and kicked the dice across the sidewalk. Arm & Hammer shoved Pernell three feet out of his vicinity. "Why the fuck you bickin' my dice fo' nigga?!"

Pernell's color rushed back into his face. "Fuck yo dice, you niggas over here pussyfooting on your hands and knees while my own relative just tried to knock me off!"

It got so quiet you could've heard one of those big face hundreds in Arm & Hammer's fist land on the sidewalk. Everyone around the dice game including myself knew that Pernell's relative was from the other side, and he was also OG P-Nutt's son. That was the same guy Pernell pulled his pistol out on a week earlier.

Boguard was the first to break the silence. "Fuck that nigga, then, on Piiiirrru!"

Arm & Hammer agreed. "On the set. Fuck blood."

Fly nodded in the direction of the big homies that were sixty yards away in the parking lot. Red, P-Nutt, and a couple of other older homies were still posted in the parking lot next to Red's cherry '64 Impala. Fly's voice still didn't have enough base in it to be heard past our circle. "We gotta wait 'til they leave before we can put this together."

Boguard wasn't in the mood for anything passive, he threw his 24oz of Old English across the park. "What the fuck you mean we wait?!"

Slim tried to calm Boguard down. "You know why, nigga." He looked over Boguard's shoulder to make sure they weren't being noticed. " Because P-Nutt will try to stall this shit out. Especially if he hears it was his son and nephew."

I tried recalling the story Fly told me about Pernell and his relative.

"You remember the nigga Pernell pulled the whop out on the other day? That was his relative, B Braze. That's the OG homie, P-Nutt's son and Pernell is his nephew. When Pernell and his relative were about six, Pernell's pops was murked leaving Green Cat Liquor. Story has it he walked up on some niggas in the parking lot looking to buy some water and one of them turned around and left his noodles lying next to him in the street. Ever since then, P-Nutt has taken in Pernell like he was his own son. His relative, B Braze, hates that shit."

Slim's voice broke my train of thought. "Blood, the big homies just smashed."

Arm & Hammer took a knee in the middle of our huddle. "Check it out. We all know what needs to brack." Arm & Hammer pointed at Slim. "You, my nigga, we need you to get two models; you know the kind. Something dark and off the radar." Slim sparked his blunt and nodded. "Meet us at the dungeon in an hour."

Arm & Hammer made a gesture with his head for Slim to leave and Slim slipped away from the huddle, his jet-black complexion blending in with the shadows. Everything was moving at the speed of light and I didn't have time to catch my breath. Pernell stood in the center of us all, his face still chalked with the white dust from the concrete wall that must've exploded when the bullets hit it.

Arm & Hammer made eye contact with each one of us that circled Pernell. "Remember the first rule, proper preparation prevents poor performance. That means we need to find out where these niggas finna be at, and fast."

Arm & Hammer's words found their way to Boguard who hadn't stopped pacing since Pernell kicked the dice. "I know exactly where blood and them niggas bick it. They be over at that bitch Darlene house. My relative drove me past there one day. Darlene stays in that pink house on 43rd, right behind Humberto's."

The area Boguard was talking about didn't ring a bell to me but it didn't matter because Pernell and Arm & Hammer knew what he was talking about. Both of their faces lit up with that information. Arm & Hammer walked my way but stopped at Fly, who was next to me. He leaned his head close enough to Fly's right ear and spoke but his whisper wasn't really a whisper. I heard everything he said but I just couldn't understand it. It was a mixture of some sort of Pig Latin and slang, but Fly understood it all because he excused himself from the huddle and got on his phone.

Watching everyone listen to Arm & Hammer was interesting. He resembled a general commanding his troops for battle. All the times I hung out with Pernell, Arm & Hammer never had much to say. He would stare at me mostly, watching my every move. That's it. I once overheard him tell Pernell that he didn't trust me because I used to live in Point Loma with all the white folks.

Arm & Hammer tapped Boguard on the chest with the back of his hand. "Since you know where the bitch stays when we smash over there we will follow you." Boguard listened to his instructions. He finally seemed at peace now that a plan was being devised. He was with all the shenanigans and everyone knew it.

Pernell made it a point to grab Boguard's attention. "Look, Ru, no kamikaze shit. The first objective is to complete the mission and the second is to get away." Boguard brushed Pernell's wisdom to the side. "Makes no sense in putting in work and getting smashed for it. We don't want the street fame; we just want the mission completed and for us not to get caught. Bottom line."

All of sudden Arm & Hammer sprung himself onto the tabletop, as P-Nutt did earlier. His athletic frame carved out space in the night sky as he fired off his warnings before our mission. "If any of you niggas ain't ready for this type of shit, then go the fuck home." He paused and I felt like his words were directed at me. "I don't expect all you niggas to put in some work, this ain't for everybody. But if you do go on this mission and then snitch, nobody in your family is off the table. We gon' knock off, you, ya momma, ya daddy, and whoever the fuck else you think you love. On Piru! So make sure this is in you and not on you."

By the time Arm & Hammer stepped off the table and back into our mini huddle, I watched a handful of niggas who were on the outside walk away. I didn't know what they were about to do but I figured I should follow suit. I took one step outside the huddle then Arm & Hammer's voice rang me back in. "Where in the fuck do you think you goin' new nigga? I wasn't talking to you." He pulled his riders out of his back pocket and threw them at my chest. "You're bomin'!"

Arm & Hammer's instructions hit me harder than his fist did earlier. What the fuck did he expect me to do? I didn't own a gun, I ain't never been on a mission, plus I didn't even know what house or girl Boguard was talking about. I didn't know what the hell to do but it didn't matter because like everyone else, he told me what I was supposed to do. "Deshaun, you finna smash with Boguard."

Boguard almost flipped his lid. A vein that ran from the base of his hairline down to his neck started to pulsate. I don't know if he realized it or not but I didn't like him as much as he didn't like me. Boguard ran up in my face for the third time today, his finger poking my chest. I was about to give him a quick jab to back him up but Pernell snatched him by the back of his shirt and pulled him away. Boguard spun one hundred eighty degrees and squared off with Pernell, his voice echoing through the park. "The fuck I am! Blood just got put on, I ain't fucking with a nigga like that."

Arm & Hammer didn't wait for another outburst from Boguard, he lunged from behind me and wrapped his forearms around his neck and squeezed. Boguard's 6'2" frame flopped around as he tried wiggling his way out of Arm & Hammer's forearms, but the more he moved the more he looked like a pretzel.

"Look nigga," Arm & Hammer applied more pressure around Boguard's neck. "We all finna meet at the dungeon in an hour so shut the fuck up and I will B you there." Arm & Hammer kept his arm wrapped around Boguard's neck for another half minute before releasing him. "And by the way, the new nigga is smashing with you, bottom line."

Chapter 20

The dungeon was nothing more than a garage but it reminded me of Bruce Wayne's Batcave because of all the different artillery we were able to stock up on before we left for our mission. That was where Arm & Hammer also told Pernell he had to sit this one out. He said because he was as hot as fish grease it would be best for him and his girl to go to the movies for the rest of the night so he can have an alibi for what was about to happen.

Pernell wasn't too fond of that plan but by the time Slim came back with the stolen cars, Pernell was already gone. Riding down the freeway in a stolen car on my first mission with a guy I fought twice earlier, was the last thing I imagined when Slim called me and told me to meet Pernell at the park. Honestly, I don't know what I've gotten myself into but it seems too late to back out now.

In the pocket of my hoodie, the .38 felt like a brass paperweight in my hand. My fingers found their way around the grooves of the soft, sticky rubber that stuck to my palm. Other than the Nerf guns I've gotten for Christmas, I've never held a real gun a day in my life.

Arm & Hammer said this would be the easiest to shoot since there wasn't much kick in a .38.

Boguard sat behind the steering wheel at a ninety degree angle, both his hands were positioned ten and two. His Philadelphia Phillies hat sat in his lap and he kept his head straight. Arm & Hammer told us to look as square as possible while driving over there and Boguard was doing a damn good job at that. The palm trees that lined the freeway resembled God's paintbrushes.

In my side mirror, I kept checking to make sure we didn't lose Fly and Arm & Hammer. They were two car lengths behind us like they said they would be. Fly must've leaned the passenger seat all the way to the backseat because the only shadow I saw in the car was Arm & Hammers.

We were only a hundred yards away from exiting the freeway when Boguard told me to pay attention. He made a right at the light where the Jack In The Box was located. I think that street was 43rd because within a blink of an eye on my left was the taco shop Boguard mentioned at the park. The building looked like it just received a fresh coat of yellow paint and bright red stripes to match. That was my landmark to start looking for Darlene's pink house and it wasn't hard to spot because B Braze's Monte Carlo was parked out front next to the curb.

Without me knowing my hand became so tightly gripped around the .38 it started to cramp the closer we got to the taco shop. If the hoodie wasn't already cinched underneath my chin, Boguard would've seen the sweat dripping down the side of my temples. The sweet aroma from tortillas being dropped in hot oil was starting to make my stomach more nauseous than it already was.

Boguard turned the radio down, let his foot off the gas, and nodded his head left so I could notice the two shadows hovering over the trunk of the Monte Carlo. The two of them were too busy eating and laughing to notice us making a right onto Keller. "Did you bthe short nigga with braids and green shirt?" I nodded. "That's blood we finna knock off. That's B Braze bitch ass."

B Braze was an exact replica of Pernell. The way he used his hand gestures as he was talking, to the way he bent his back leg slightly when he stood. It feels like we're going after Pernell in a sense. I cleared my throat. "And, who's the other person with him?" I wanted to make sure we weren't shooting any innocent bystanders.

Boguard took the extra long Newport out of the box and put a lighter to the tip of it. The cherry of the cigarette gave off enough light to see his face. He pointed to the shorter one. "That bitch ass nigga next to him with the red hair and freckles, that's Buster Rob faggot ass. Blood's bitch ass used to live in the set before Arm & Hammer laid that demo down on him." The image of Arm & Hammer teeing off on Buster Rob that first day I went with Pernell to the center of the apartments flashed on the screen of my mind.

Boguard cocked the .40cal, placed it on his lap, and pointed to the tail lights that were parked two car lengths ahead of us. "Get ready because when the homies get out, we're following."

I didn't move a muscle. All I could hear was my own heartbeat; I could even hear Boguards nervous breaths between each time he sucked on the cigarette. Two sets of shadows exited the car and moved towards the taco shop. The red bandana Pernell gave me before he left the dungeon was folded into a triangle on my lap. I pulled my hoodie down and covered the bottom half of my face.

My eyes stayed glued on Arm & Hammer and Fly who were crouched next to a set of stairs at the end of the block. Fifty yards ahead of them Buster Rob walked into the taco shop and left B Braze sitting on the trunk of the car alone. Arm & Hammer sprung from behind the shadows and sprinted towards the middle of the street with Fly close on his hip. The .44 Magnum being held with both hands, Fly started barking first.

The first bullet bit its way through Buster Rob's cheek who was walking out of the taco shop with a brown bag of food in his hand. Chunks of whatever is supposed to be in someone's head splattered against the wall next to him. Arm & Hammer stood at the double yellow lines in the middle of the street with the twin .45's in his hands firing at B Braze who jumped off the trunk trying to find cover behind his car.

Boguard's arm shot across my line of sight and pointed to a figure running out of the pink house that B Braze was parked out front of. Running down the driveway was a mocha-complected girl with nothing on but a black lace bra and a pair of green booty shorts, pointing at what looked like a Tec 9 directly at Arm & Hammer and Fly.

I don't know what got in my soul for me to jump out of my seat and run to the middle of the street with a .38 in my hand, aiming at the half-naked girl but something did. Whatever it was, it was instinctual. I shut my left eye like I've seen in movies to get a better focus and aimed at the giant four-leaf clover tattooed in the middle of her chest and squeezed.

Chapter 21

—◼••◼—

Day 44:

The scream of pure terror when the bullet ripped through Darlene's cleavage was still tattooing my ear drums seven days later. I've heard screams from teammates who've broken their legs on the football field but hers was in a different league. It grabbed at the skin above my heart and sliced it in half to embed itself into my DNA. It didn't matter how many times I tried showering I couldn't scrub the memory out of me.

I needed to talk to someone and the only person that came to mind was my dad but he was never home for me to talk with. Since moving here I've only seen him two times, if that. He tends to leave for work before I get up in the morning and gets home after I've passed out from drinking and smoking all day. Plus it wouldn't matter anyway. How do you tell your parents that you're having nightmares because you've shot a woman through her chest and witnessed another person's brain fly out the back of his head?

Chapter 22

—◆••◆—

The light taps from the tips of my mom's fingernails along my bedroom door made me stuff my journal as far as I could under my bed. There is no way on God's green earth did I need her to find my journal and read it. Soon I'm going to have to find a better place to hide it but for today this will have to do. Her light taps on my door in the morning were a reminder that breakfast was ready. It's been a pleasure eating with her for the last week but I know soon I will be running back outside with the homies once the coast clears.

By the time I made it to the kitchen, the table was already set with my favorite breakfast; bacon, two eggs over-easy, a slice of Wonder bread buttered from end to end with a full glass of strawberry Kool-aid. Honestly, this treatment was normal on my birthday but not on a random Sunday, but I sure wasn't going to mention anything about it to her. My mom walked from the stove and around the table and kissed me on top of my curly head and moved into the TV room. "What was the kiss for mom?"

Her silence made me stop chewing and swivel around in my chair. The crow's feet around the corners of her eyes were starting to collect water from tears forming. Her voice, which was normally smoother than a baby's bottom, sounded like Bobbies from my seventh-grade calculus class. "Son, I'm s...." My fork slipped out of my hand. "I'm sorry. I'm sorry that we had to move and take you away from everything you've ever known. I feel horrible that you won't be able to graduate with Alex and Lee and that we took you away from your football dreams. And I don't know if you've talked to your dad yet but he feels the same way too. I've noticed how it has been taking a toll on you over this last week. You've hardly come out of your room, you barely eat your favorite foods that I cook for you and you're constantly looking out the window to see if your dad is coming up the stairs."

Me hiding things from my mom was never a strong suit so I didn't know why I could start now but I'm glad she believes it's over my pops and not what I did at the taco shop. She dragged her palms across her face and her mascara smeared down her plump cheeks. She walked to me and pulled my head into her chest. "I love you son. I promise we won't be here long. Your dad is trying hard to get another job and when he does we will move back to Point Loma. Just promise me while we're here you will stay far away from all the nonsense that's going on outside these four walls."

Chapter 23

It's been eight days and still no word from anyone that was with me that night. Arm & Hammer said for us to lay low until the smoke cleared but the isolation was slowly starting to pick at my sanity. Any footsteps I heard coming up the stairs had me out the blinds of my room hoping it wasn't the SWAT team coming to kick in the door and arrest me. My mom was right. I've hardly left my room let alone eat, but how could I when my stomach was constantly in my throat?

The eight-by-ten frame that housed the picture of me shaking Drew Brees hand at the Martin Bayless Football Camp fell from off my dresser when the cordless phone rang. That probably was the first noise I've heard in my room in the last eight days other than my thoughts. "Hello?" I whispered into the receiver.

"What's brackin' D?" I kept quiet as Pernell started to rattle off what he's been up to for the last few days. Pernell's nonchalant attitude about his endeavors always brought a smile to my face. There was something about the way he was able to compartmentalize danger and risk and not allow it to affect his mood that brought a sense of ease over me. He continued with a story of how he and Fly beat up some guy in all green clothing for trying to skate through the apartments to visit his grandma. Then his voice shifted. "The homies are at the green box. Make sure you're there in eight minutes." Then the phone went dead.

All the reasons for me not to leave my room came flooding in as if my body sensed something my brain couldn't see. At times it's wise to let the feeling of fear educate you but this wasn't one of those times. I threw on a pair of 501's and a white tee and headed out the house. Ms. Balboa, the apartment manager who lived underneath us, was outside sweeping the courtyard. There was something about her stares that made the hair on my arms cringe.

When I made it to the green box, everyone from the other night was already there. Fly and Boguard were draped in all red while Arm & Hammer, no matter the occasion, stayed with his hoodie over his head. Everyone from the other night was there plus Slim and Pernell. Pernell nodded his head for me to keep walking and follow him to the splintered bench in front of the pool enclosure twenty yards ahead.

Other than a half-cocked smile inching across his face he was emotionless. It was like our conversation over the phone never happened. Everything he was doing was real straight edge and dry. I couldn't gauge what was about to happen. He hiked one foot on the bench like the pirate on the Captain Morgan bottle and pointed for me to take a seat on the other end. I know I'm new to this but me sitting and him standing didn't seem like the best idea. This was the same spot where they jumped Buster Rob and I don't want that same outcome.

Pernell laughed at my reluctance. "Sit cha scary ass down, nigga, ain't no one finna do shit to you." I tried acting like that wasn't the case but he knew. He always knew. I wiped the Flaming Hot Cheeto crumbs that were left on the edge of the bench and sat down. "I heard how you performed the other night, they said you did yo' thang. I wanna congratulate you little nigga."

Who in the hell told Pernell? Don't get me wrong, Pernell's my best friend but Arm & Hammers instructions were clear, don't tell a fucking soul. He said the fewer people who knew about that night meant less chances of someone tellin'. You can't tell what you don't know.

The pitter-patter of naked feet running across concrete got me to turn around. It was a little Mexican boy no older than five chasing a colorful soccer ball that escaped the gated pool area behind me. Pernell stopped the ball with his foot then started dribbling it on his knee before kicking it the kid's way. Pernell's shoulder slumped forward, his hands started fidgeting with the blunt behind his ear. "You remember Krystal?" I had to think about it for a brief second but her round face and even rounder butt came to mind. "Well, last night she told me she's pregnant, and it's mine."

What I expected to be excitement turned out to be the opposite. His brow made a sharp V in the middle of his forehead as his strides marched him back and forth until they came to a halt in front of me. He was looking my way but his gaze was focused on something behind him like he didn't want to look me in my eyes. "D, I know I'm supposed to be happy but on the set, I love the turf too much to love anything else right now."

How can a father say that about his child? That he loves something greater than the thing that came from him. That thought process shouldn't surprise me because that seems like the approach my own dad has taken with this new job. He has been giving them sixteen-hour days and me and my mom zero. I took the blunt Pernell was handing me. "Pernell, it doesn't have to be an either-or type of thing. You can choose to love both."

"Look, D, in this here shit we call bangin' you can't serve two masters. It is an either-or type of situation. Either you give the set your all or you don't. Because once you're on the fence and not willing to die for the set or go to the penitentiary for this, that's when you start making the wrong decisions. That's why niggas be snitching now because they done lost their sense of loyalty. That's why I don't want Krystal to have this baby. I know where my loyalty stands. I'm all in my nigga.."

Standing up I was eye to eye with Pernell and any confusion that I thought I saw a second ago had vanished. He made his stance and there was no chance of me changing it now. His commitment was to the homies and the set, so I made one with him. My right hand transformed into a capital P, as he gave me when I arrived at the green box earlier. "You don't have to say any more Pernell. I get it. Just so you know, I'm all in too."

Chapter 24

Today is the day that Pernell and Fly have been hyping up for the last two weeks. It's San Diego's Annual Puerto Rican Day Festival at Mission Beach. See, me. I've never been personally. I've only seen what was reported on the news later that night and if I use my mom's words, there seemed to be a lot of riff-raff at those festivals. Honestly, the only time I've been to Mission Beach was a couple of years back on the Fourth of July when my parents allowed me to go with Alex and his family, as long as I promised not to make going back there a habit.

When we lived in Point Loma my mom said that Mission Beach is where all the beach bums, alcoholics and tourists went. She preferred going to the beach on Coronado Island. She said there was something magical about the sand next to Hotel Del Coronado that when she stuck her toes in the pearly white sand it felt like she was getting a manicure. I, on the other hand, hated the drive over the bridge. It sucked. It was too tall and the lanes were too narrow. I always kept my eyes shut every time we crossed it. Today I wouldn't have to worry about any of that because I'm going to where I promised my mom I wouldn't be going.

Pernell, Fly, and Arm & Hammer were out front waiting for me to hurry up. One of the benefits of Pernell dating Krystal was that her dad bought her a brand new gold Lexus GS 300 and Pernell was always driving it. As much as he drove it, anyone that didn't know him would have thought it was his. The bass from the trunk let me know that he was out front. By the time I made it outside and to the car, Fly was rushing me. "Hurry the fuck up, nigga, and hop ya ass in the car. You finna have us miss all the bitches wit cha slow ass."

The drive was about forty-five minutes because of the traffic but it was all worth it once we entered Mission Beach. What I saw looked like those pictures that were on a postcard you could get at SeaWorld or something. The number of beautiful women walking around in bikinis was something I couldn't keep my eyes off of. They were everywhere. Every color, shade and creed were trotting around, flaunting what the good Lord gave them.

Pernell pulled into the parking lot west of the roller coaster at Belmont Park. I couldn't tell what my mom meant by riff-raff. Did she mean the scantily clothed women parading around in bikinis that looked like dental floss? Or the groups of gang members hanging out in different sections that qualified her title? The only difference that mattered to me, that I saw at Mission Beach compared to Coronado, was that it was full of life, energy and a hell of a lot more color. And I'm talking about people, not shirts.

Fly rolled down the passenger window to get a better view of a chocolate goddess,

making her way through the parking lot towards a group of 30 or so guys posted in the grass next to the playground barbecuing. If I wouldn't have known that Snoop Dog was from Long Beach I would've bet all the money in my pocket that the group she was walking to was him and his homies. Up until that point I've never seen that much blue in one area a day in my life.

There was a gigantic blue bandana clipped from one leg of the EZ Up to the other and it covered the entire back of the tent. Little kids in blue bandana house shoes chased each other around with water guns having the time of their lives, while some guys that looked my age sat around the plastic tables playing what looked like Dominoes. Everyone either had on some Milwaukee Brewers attire or were blued up from head to toe.

Pernell passed the blunt over his shoulder to me and nodded his head to another group of individuals congregating next to a slew of muscle cars to the left of the parking lot. Each car had its own personality but there was a common theme to them all, each one had some sort of green entangled in them, either in the interior or the paint but every last one of them had its share of green.

Arm & Hammer snatched the blunt out of my hand and pointed in the direction of the muscle cars. I followed the sightline of his finger to a white 71' Chevelle with the green patchwork interior where I saw exactly what he pointing at, it was him, the nigga we tried to kill last week. B Braze stood amongst his homies laughing like he didn't have a worry in the world, like we didn't go over to the taco shop a week ago and try to kill him.

Pernell must've finally seen what we saw and almost broke the handle trying to get out the door. Fly had to harness Pernell by his shoulders. "Bick it nigga, this ain't the time nor the place." Pernell elbowed Fly's hand that was holding his shirt but Fly wouldn't let go. "Relax P Funk. A little broad I know put me up on where B Braze has been hiding out at. We can get blood tonight. Just bick back and be bool for right now."

Pernell's body swayed back and forth as he sat in front of me. The vein that ran from his forehead alongside his temple down to his jaw pulsated as he tried calming himself down. He reached underneath his front seat and pulled the .45 caliber that I haven't seen since that day we were on the corner and switched the safety off and stuffed it in his waist.

Arm & Hammer took another hit of the blunt before he tossed it out the window and slid himself forward so that he was in between the two front seats. He swatted away Fly's hand that still had a tiny grip of Pernell's shirt and leaned close enough to Pernell that only they knew what was said amongst each other.

Fly's annoying ringtone broke up the tension inside the car. The falsetto pitch of Slim on the other end of the phone was loud enough for me to hear him from the backseat. According to Slim, he and the homies were already functioning at the tables west of the bathrooms and if we didn't hurry the fuck up we would miss all the bad bitches they had with them.

Being outside the car and in the mix was different than being a spectator from inside a bulk of metal on four wheels. The Reggaeton that filled the air commanded every woman walking in front of us to sway their hips in rhythm. The sweetened air from street vendors along the sidewalk who were caramelizing baby bananas on their heavy iron skillets made my mouth water while we walked towards Slim and the homies.

Other than going on that mission with Fly, Boguard, and Arm & Hammer last week and being around Pernell these last couple days, I haven't seen anyone since the day I got jumped in at the park. P-Nutt stood next to Slim, watching him blow smoke out the opposite end of his blunt into the mouth of a chic who made J Lo look like a bum. Her body was painted with red and blue to match the Puerto Rico flag, her two long french braids hung neatly over her clavicle and they were just the right width to cover nipples God glued to her dainty breasts.

I wish I could've stopped with the rest of the homies and enjoyed the festivities but I had to piss so bad I could almost taste it. The pint of Hennessy we drank on the way here made me beeline straight to the manilla brick building that housed the urinals. One thing about beach bathrooms is that they always had that one extra-long urinal that stretched about twenty feet long against the wall and we were all supposed to stand next to each other with our dicks in our hand and piss. Luckily this time it was only me.

A familiar voice pierced my eardrums "Now, what's craccin', cuz?"

My heart almost dropped in the urinal before me. I stuffed my dick back into my pants as fast as I could and turned around and squared off. "What's brackin'?"

"Oh, is that right? It's what's brackin' now?"

Standing in front of me was Tiny Blue Rocc. He must've been with the group of guys in blue by the playground. I haven't seen him since my mom stopped allowing me to visit my dad's brother's house two summers ago when a twelve-year-old boy was gunned down in front of his house on 39th and Hilltop. Tiny Blue Rocc's eyes said more than his body language. "So, you stop comin' to your uncle's house and move to the other side of town and now you start bangin' my nigga? Ain't chu a little late, cuz?"

I kept my mouth shut.

Tiny Blue Rocc hiked his pants over his waist and looked me up and down. I knew what that meant. That was the same thing the ese's did right before they swung at Pernell and me at the trolley. I balled my fist up ready for whatever he wanted to do.

"So what the fuck they call you then cuz?" I didn't say a word, I just watched his shoulders like Pernell taught me those days in the garage during our boxing lessons. He took another step closer. "All of a sudden the cat gotcha tongue, nigga? Where the fuck you think you from then D?"

He was right, where am I from? Even though I've already gone on a mission, I've yet to tell anyone where I was from. A voice inside of me I've never heard jumped out. "I'm from Piru, nigga, that's where I'm from!"

That didn't seem to bother Tiny Blue Rocc one bit, it even drew a chuckle out of him. "Is that right, D?" He laughed a little harder this time. "All of sudden, huh? When you used to come visit your uncle in the set, you were squarer than a box of cereal and now, you're bangin'? I guess nigga. But checc it out D, I just came to see what was hatnin' wit my old-school potna, but I see now that you ain't the same old-school nigga as before. Just remember, this ain't no game. You better know whatchu gettin' yourself into before you get cha' self murked. C safe out here, cuz."

And like that, Tiny Blue Rocc bent the corner and he was out of the bathroom. No dap, no half-hug with a handshake, no nothing. It was just me, alone, contemplating his words and wondering if what he said was true. Am I really not that old-school nigga anymore just because I'm from Piru? Why would that change our relationship?

Running my hands under the leaking faucet I kept shaking my head trying to rid myself of any doubt Tiny Blue Rocc was trying to plant. There was nothing that was different about me, I was still the same old Deshaun. He's the one who's changed, running up on me asking me where I'm from.

When I stepped out of the bathroom I could feel it, something had changed. It felt like that night, that night at the taco shop, the night when the air was paralyzed between tension and unforgivable sin. Swallowing another ounce of oxygen became a fight with my anxiety but I was up for the battle because I had to be, it was going down. The homies were no longer at the table having a good time. They were in the middle of a melee. P-Nutt was in the sand next to the tables pulling Slim to his feet, almost tearing his collar off his shirt as he tried dragging him to safety. Arm & Hammer was to the right of them, his pistol slamming into the side of someone's dreads as he pinned him against the light pole, while Fly and Pernell were back to back and surrounded by B Braze and a nest of green shirts. My heart felt like it was going to explode watching what was happening in front of me. My legs wanted to keep me safe but standing around wasn't an option. Let's face it. At some point I knew I had to run towards the chaos so that's exactly what I did.

Tiny Blue Rocc

Chapter 25

—◆◦◆—

There hasn't been a single night when I rest my head on my pillow that I don't see Lil Blue Rocc's face. It's the same thing every night, him sitting on the curb in front of my granny house, his legs kicked out in front of him, his feet crossed at the ankles waiving a picture in his left hand that I couldn't quite make out and him chanting under his breath. Each step closer the picture begins to develop. It's the picture of me and him when we were at the group home together five years ago standing behind the tool shed where it all started, where it became official, where I took that oath and became Tiny Blue Rocc and my brother's keeper.

The devil on my shoulder couldn't keep his mouth shut and I couldn't take my hand off the butt of my .50 caliber stuffed in my dickies. Watching a bunch of slob niggas fight wasn't my thing but what was, was finally seeing the bitch ass nigga who killed Lil Blue Rocc. Fortyseven yards and a gang of fuccin' innocent bystanders were the only things that kept cuz alive.

I've been to every spot he's been to in the last three weeks but he kept slipping through my fingers. I almost had him last Sunday when my cousin, Aisha, called and told me she saw him leaving the house on St. Rita's with his granny but by the time I got there, I was a couple of minutes behind. But today, I didn't have to worry about that 'cause it looks like God's intervening in my search, who else can hand a nigga over on a silver platter like this?

Cowboy's voice blanketed the devil in my ear. "Keep that muthafucka tucced cuz. We ain't tryin' to catch a life case my nigga. We're playing Chess not Checkers."

Cowboy was right but I couldn't fuck off this blessing that God was giving me right now. Cuz gots to die today. I took my hand off the butt of my pistol and ran down the plan to Cowboy. "You're right cuz, then this is what we finna do. We are gonna park up the street in the parking lot at the Bahia and when cuz and 'em pass the light we're gonna follow. When he gets on the 805, that's when we will leave his noodles in his lap."

Chapter 26

It's been two fucking hours and cuz still ain't left the parking lot. I've wiped down every bullet no less than a hundred times. Cowboy always kept the big boy in his trunk for occasions like this, he just didn't give a fucc. I pushed the extended clip into the AR-15 and laid it across my lap as Cowboy fired up the engine. Half of the sun was tucked behind the Pacific by the time the Monte Carlo stopped at the dead light catty-corner to where we were parked.

Knocking a nigga off wasn't anything new to us, this was my dog, we've been on countless decorated missions together so we knew the protocol. Two car lengths behind and never in the same lane. When and if he changes lanes, we wait ten seconds before we move and never use a blinker. Our light turned green and we kept our distance as he headed to the freeway.

Cowboy lit the rest of the Newport and passed it my way. If you've ever smelled embalming fluid before, then know, you will never mistake it for a regular Newport. The Formaldehyde traps its odor in the layers of your tongue and you can taste it just by smelling it. The sugary fumes embalmed my chest with revenge. It's been twenty-one days since the cig homie was smoked in front of me and that's twenty-one days too long.

Cowboy took the stick back and pulled on it so hard that the cherry burned down to the filter. The haze of smoke sitting against the windshield made it impossible for me to keep my eyes on B Braze. Cowboy's voice cut through the smoke as he flicked the butt out the window. "It looks like cuz is exiting. You ready?"

The brake lights in front of us were our homing beacons. The more pressure he applied the brighter they became. The traffic light switched green to yellow then red, as the Monte Carlo crawled to a complete stop. The dope fiend jumping up and down on the corner blended in with the shadows the closer we got to the Monte Carlo. B Braze's outline was all I could make out as we approached. A light from his dashboard matched the embossed green SS stitching on the inlay of the passenger's headrest.

My eyes were like lenses to a camera, every blink was a new imprint over an old memory. I needed to capture every detail so I can scrub my memory of Lil Blue Rocc dying in my arms. Every night without fail I relive that scene in my head. Lil Blue Rocc being lifted off his feet, flying past me ten feet, then dying in my arms was on a constant loop in my head. It's like a migraine headache that never eases up.

We were ten feet away, then eight, then four, then Cowboy was pulling alongside the back right fender of the Monte Carlo. I thought I would get more satisfaction in seeing B Braze's face before I pulled the trigger than actually seeing his soul leave his body, but the crazy part was I liked them both. Before pulling the trigger B Braze slightly opened his mouth, a smirk stretched across his cheeks. His eyes were fixed as if he was looking at something four feet behind my head. "What's craccin now cuz?"

The clock was ticking, my time was limited. Every wasted minute was a betrayed promise to Lil Blue Rocc. My surroundings blurred into a new reality as I held my finger on the trigger. His head snapped forward and the blood from the holes in his chest came tumbling out his mouth. His frame no longer sat in a ninety-degree angle as he took every bullet I had. His once tough body was now slumped forward over the steering wheel matching the green bandana that hung over his rearview mirror. The melodic tune from the steering wheel crying sounded like Reaper's trumpets congratulating me, but it wasn't over just yet.

I tossed the empty AR in the backseat and ran over to the Monte Carlo. He was breathing but only shallow gasps. He was dying but not quick enough. Seconds passed before I grabbed his head and looked him in his face. Blood flooded through his eyes as I pressed my .40 caliber against the center of his forehead. His eyes shut as I whispered the last words he would ever hear.

"This one is for the homie, cuz!"

Deshaun

Chapter 27

B oguard stood in the garage next to the deep freezer and inhaled on the Swisher Sweet. "Who do you know that will drop their son for the set?"

The homies that were gathered around laughed but Bogurard was right, that was some cold-blooded shit. I ain't never seen anything like that. Even though my pops and I are not as close as we once were I could never see him doing some shit like that to me. After P-Nutt left Slim in the sand he ran towards Pernell and B Braze who were going toe to toe in the middle of all the chaos. The two were like gladiators fighting in the coliseum. P-Nutt's old legs began to pick up speed as he made a straight line for his son. B Braze's back was turned when P-Nutt came running with his elbow and forearm held high and connected to the back of his son's neck.

P-Nutt took the blunt from Boguard and addressed the garage. "Fuck that nigga, he ain't my son no mo'. That little brosstown nigga needed that shit. He's lucky I didn't take my belt off and start whooping his little-ass in front of everybody." P-Nutt pivoted towards Boguard and got within spitting distance. "Since you're doing a whole bunch of laughing right now, nigga, I don't remember beeing you in the mix."

The garage went silent and P-Nutt's charismatic smile vanished while he waited for Boguard to answer. All of us in the garage looked at each other with a blank stare. I don't remember seeing Boguard once the funk popped off. I think all of us that were at the beach had the same thought. Where was he? He wasn't with me when I ran to help Fly when he was getting jumped by three niggas. He wasn't next to Slim and P-Nutt when they initially got surrounded nor was he by Slim when he got dope fiend. I didn't see him helping Arm & Hammer pistol-whipping anybody and he damn sure wasn't next Pernell in the middle of the chaos.

P-Nutt turned and addressed Arm & Hammer. "Did you p this nigga in action?" Arm & Hammer shook his head no. Then P-Nutt looked at Pernell. "Nephew, did you p 'em?" Pernell looked in the opposite direction and didn't answer his uncle. Then he turned to me. "New blood, where was this nigga at when we were chunkin' 'em?"

I didn't want to be a snitch but I knew I couldn't lie to P-Nutt. What he was asking was a valid question.

Where was Boguard? I cleared my throat so when I spoke up P-Nutt could hear me. "I don't know where he was at, big homie. I didn't p him in the mix at all."

P-Nutt didn't say another word and he didn't have to, his actions were loud enough. A right hook to Boguards unexpected kidney dropped him in his spot. Boguard laid on the cement floor of the garage trying to catch his breath through what sounded like a straw. P-Nutt hovered over Boguard and looked at the rest of us. "You niggas better not ever do some bomedy-ass shit like blood just pulled off. Ain't no bickin' it when the funks brackin', period!"

Red emerged from the side of the garage. His demeanor always came off to me as very nonchalant but it was the perfect balance to P-Nutt's authoritarian style. The scar along his face always made it seem like he was smiling. He looked down at Boguard hugging himself on the ground then he looked to P-Nutt still hovering above him. "Nutt, you bool?"

P-Nutt grabbed his plastic cup and walked over Boguard. "Yea, I'm bool, blood. But blood right there needs to be DP'd." P-Nutt didn't say another word. He tossed his plastic cup into the overgrown grass and walked to the side of the house.

Red glanced over at Boguard still trying to catch his breath. "Listen up, you little niggas." We all took a step closer to Red so we could hear exactly what he had to say. "What blood did was bomedy, ain't no question about it, but that doesn't erase all the work blood has put in for the set. So don't worry about DP'ing blood right now, just get him to the gates and then we'll have a meeting on it tomorrow." Red shot each one of us the P, before he went into the house.

Watching Boguard getting in the car with Slim and heading home made me think about one of my dad's favorite quotes he used to say during our Saturday morning football film sessions in the garage. Regardless of whether I had a great play on the field or if I had a mental lapse and blew it, his response would always be the same "remember son, you're only as good as your last play." In this instance my dad was right, it didn't matter how much "work" Boguard put in for the set, he was only as good as his last play and unfortunately for him, his last play wasn't a good one. It amazes me how he was so quick to fight me the day I walked up to the park but was nowhere to be found when we were in the middle of the melee. Maybe it's easier to fight someone who looks like me rather than someone who looks like they've been fighting their whole life. Whatever it was, I know I don't ever want to be hit by P-Nutt the way Boguard was.

The garage was starting to thin out. The only ones left hanging were Fly, Arm & Hammer, Pernell, myself, and P-Nutt being that it was his house. Standing next to Fly meant that you are always next in rotation but I was already high as a giraffe's pussy. I couldn't get any higher. Fly smoked as much weed as he sold but I was always wondering if he sold weed just to smoke or to make money. What I did know was, I've never smoked this much weed in my life. The only time I used to smoke was when Alex, Lee, and I would ride our bikes to Ocean Beach pier late at night so we could try to catch some lobster. Whenever one of us caught something we knew we hit the lottery because that meant Lee's mom would cook it for us in her San Diego Reader award-winning lobster bisque. The sweetness of the lean lobster meat wrapped with the creamy taste of the heavy whipping cream dashed with cayenne pepper and her homemade creole seasoning always made my taste buds explode.

I kept my eyelids shut as I hit the blunt trying not to forget the memories of a life that I knew I'll never live again. Now I think I understand why everyone smokes on a regular basis, probably because we are all trying to remember the good times before the thieving, the melee's, and shootings. When life had no worries other than getting up, getting dressed, and going outside to hang out with friends.

Pernell's tap on my shoulder brought me back to reality. "Pass the blunt, Deshaun. You're over there with your eyes closed making love to that muthafucka. Do that shit at home with your own blunt; not here, nigga."

I laughed right along with everyone else that was in the garage. I bet I looked dumb as shit with my eyes closed holding the blunt. P-Nutt came around from the side of the house and back into the garage. "I'm tired of hearing that square-ass name you niggas keep callin' blood."

Square-ass name? This name ain't that square and plus what else are they gonna call me? I like my name. My mom told me she named me after my great great grandfather on my dad's side who was the first American to open up a dentist office in Point Loma. Personally I didn't think there was anything wrong with my name but obviously P-Nutt did.

Fly spun himself around in the office chair like he was five years old again and gave his two cents on the topic of my name. "Since blood was out there hoggin' niggas today, how 'bout we call blood D Hogg?" Pernell and P-Nutt nodded at the same time. It looked like everyone that was in the garage was also in agreement, except for A.H., but what was new? He never liked anything anyone did or said.

Pernell was more excited than I was about my new name, and I'm glad he was because I wasn't feelin' it. But what I learned today was that P-Nutt wasn't one to get upset and if he said he was tired of my name, well then that's what it is. Pernell shot me the P and gave his confirmation. "On the set, that's what we finna call you. Since you've been comin' around, you've been wit all the activities and you ain't turned shit down." Pernell shot me the P.

He was right. Since the day he came and knocked on my door and introduced me to the homies, I've done everything that Pernell and the homies had thrown my way. From the time I jacked the bottle of liquor from Ralphs and Pernell saved my ass from the security guard, or the time we had to fight the ese's at the trolley stop over some chick Pernell was getting at. And even Arm & Hammer telling me I had to go on that mission after Pernell was almost killed, to now - the melee at the beach. I guess they were right, I've been with all the activities.

It didn't occur to me how much shit I've gotten myself into in a short amount of time but looking back on it, it sure was enough. Not in a million years could I have guessed that I would've gone from wanting to go to Penn State to maybe ending up in the State Pen. I walked out of the garage and onto the driveway. The thick air from earlier thinned itself out under the stars. Living in the city the only star visible amongst the light pollution was the one that shined the brightest.

Fly walked past me to the edge of the driveway then took a couple steps into the middle of the street and swept his head back and forth like an old grandfather clock. Coming over the crest of the hill towards us was a pair of blue headlights that almost blinded me. Fly rubbed his palms together and walked back to me, his face was etched in eagerness. "Aye D, you b them headlights?" I nodded my head wondering what extravagant story he was going to tell me next. "Those are those two bad ass bitches from the beach, the ones that wanted to buy some dro. Right before we got brackin' I had slid them my number and told'em to hit me later tonight."

Fly reached into his red Jansport backpack and took out a sandwich bag full of weed, pulled out four gram baggies then put them in his pocket. If I remember correctly he said each one of those bags cost twenty bucks. If Fly and I didn't look up when we did, the five series would have taken one of us out the way it swerved into the driveway. The mirror tint on the window made it easy for me to remember the car, it was parked close to B Braze and his homies at the beach.

The passenger door opened first and I had to catch my breath. It was Sky. I haven't seen her since the summer before last when I was visiting my dad's brother Juney. Sky looked like someone who belonged in a magazine. If Jet magazine had a beauty teen of the week then she would've been on there 52 straight times. Her neatly french manicured toes matched her rounded fingernails. She was 17 going on 27 but any grown man would've thrown her age out the window to get next to her beauty. Her golden spirals fell loosely over her shoulders and curls blended seamlessly with her raw skin which in fact made her leprechaun colored eyes even more mesmerizing. Her face was exotically constructed, the golf balls God placed in place of her cheekbones made her look like she was always smiling at life all the time. Every time I would get a chance to talk to her I always teased her about that and never once did she forget to remind me she had Cherokee in her family.

Sky stood in between the door and the car twirling a curl that hung alongside her cheek with her index finger. Her eyes were only directed at me."What are you doing over here?"

I closed the distance between us by taking one large step in her direction. I didn't want the homies to be in my business. I rested my forearms on the car door separating us and kept my eyes focused on her as I spoke. "I'm just hangin' with the homies right now," I said as I nodded my head towards the garage. "What's up with you? What brought you over here?"

Sky looked over at her friend who was exchanging four twenty dollar bills for the four grams of weed Fly had in his hand. "She's a weed head and she doesn't care what nigga has it, as long as they're hookin' it up, she's gonna get it."

I laughed as I noticed Fly reaching back into his backpack for what I'm assuming had to be another gram. I ran my eyes over Sky's sculpture and there wasn't one thing out of place. I dropped my voice two decimals so only Sky could hear what was coming out next. "I see life has been treatin' you kindly." I rubbernecked my head around the car door and glanced at her Little Debbie Hostess Cakes leaning against the side of the passenger seat. "I see you're still killin' these bitches out here with your good looks and cute feet."

Sky's cheeks raised a half-inch higher this time and I was finally able to see her pearly whites between her glossy lips. She blew a bubble the size of a tangerine before she spoke. "Boy, you tryin' hard, ain't chu?" Sky popped her gum and this time her smile didn't leave. "Anyways, I saw you out there today at the Puerto Rican Fest. I didn't know you could fight like that." The gold bangles that accompanied her wrist sounded like the wind chimes that my dad and I hung on the front porch when we were still in Point Loma. She opened the glove box and pulled out a ballpoint pen, wrote something on a crumpled receipt and handed it to me. Sky put her manicured nail between her lips, grinned and sat back in the car and closed her door. Before they backed out the driveway Sky rolled her window down and made a phone with her hands and mouthed for me to call her.

I knew what that meant, now it was up to me.

Detective Braveheart

Chapter 28

"Look at these dumb motherfuckers." My partner pointed to the dancing monkeys on the corner. He hated them as much as I did but what I hated more was how his sloppy ass kept spitting half cracked sunflower seeds on the fucking floorboard of my 64' stang.

We've been watching these fuckers for the last hour shoot dice, sell dope and hangout in front of the liquor store like the dumbass gang members they are. If my favorite confidential informant would not have called me in the wee hours of the morning informing me that something was going down today, I would have had the uniform boys come and shake all that shit up.

Whitehead poured another handful of seeds into his mouth and all but five landed on the floor mat. He looked like a damn chipmunk with both his cheeks sticking out further than his ears. "They act like nobody's watching them break the law and I don't know how they don't see us in this fucking nice ass car."

He was right, they were either stupid as fuck or blind as a bat because we are only two blocks west of their location. Protocol is to be at least four blocks away and to be in an unmarked department-issued vehicle but I never listened to protocol. If I would have listened to protocol when I was making my bones I would never be the lead detective of the Gang Suppression Unit now. There's always instances where you have to break the rules or make them up as you go because to get the conviction the rules never apply.

Flipping through a couple of pages of notes I found what I was looking for. "Our C.I. said to be on the lookout for a blue Chevrolet Caprice. He said the owner of that car is Cowboy and he was the driver that day on the freeway when B Braze was shot and murdered. So when we see the Caprice, we'll follow them and they will unknowingly lead us to the firearms."

Detective Whitehead pointed to a blue car pulling up to the south side of the liquor store. "Bingo, partner. There it is."

"I see it too, but who the fuck is that?" At our ten was a death wish walking. The red Nike's told everyone in a ten-block radius that his dumb ass didn't belong on this side of town but it looks like he didn't get the message. In my fifteen years, I've never seen anyone that bold to walk in this neighborhood with that much red on without packing some kind of heat, but the way he's smiling and walking without a worry in the fucking world with a girl on his right, I have to beg to differ.

"What the fuck do you think he's doing?"

My partner was right. What the fuck is this kid doing? There's no bulge along his waistline, or any baseball gloves wrapped around his fists like he's ready to fight, like I've seen countless other dumb ass gang members do. So what the fuck is he doing?

While his thin afro swayed with every bouncing step he took as he crossed the street, that's when it hit me. I've seen this fucker before. It was three and a half weeks ago in Paradise Hills when I was pulling out of the Jack In The Box drive-through and saw him and his partner on the corner of Alta View and Woodman. His partner had a chrome, what looked like a .45 caliber semi-automatic handgun drawn out on an individual in a green Monte Carlo. The two of them were able to flee the scene as I was running the red light.

I felt a tap on the right side of my knee. "Hey, you think we should go down there and stop him from getting murdered?"

His words lingered in the car and I could give two fucks about his concerns. The more monkeys that kill each other the less money the taxpayers have to bear for locking their guilty asses up, and it made my job easier if they were dead. All that was irrelevant because my sole attention was on Tiny Blue Rocc and his movements.

It seemed odd to me that he stood off in the back behind the pack with his arms crossed leaning against the Caprice. If he is the line pusher like my informant tagged him to be then his actions do not match. As the rest of his crew rushed to the middle of the street to jump on the dummy and his chick he sat back smiling like a proud father.

My partner slapped my arm this time with a little more force to snap me out of my trance. "You see this shit? I know we don't care about these gang members but I'm not cool with letting those heathens down there slap that young lady. She has nothing to do with any of that, she has just found herself with the wrong guy."

I turned my head away from the Caprice and watched the ass whooping Tiny Blue Rocc's crew was giving the kid in the middle of the street. For it to be four of them against him he was handling his own until a stubby kid snuck in from his blind side and hit him over the head with a glass beer bottle. I'm honestly glad he was getting this ass whooping, it left me with one last thing to do when I caught up to him. After a few stomps and kicks I shifted my attention back to Tiny Blue Rocc, but he and Cowboy and the blue Caprice were gone. They must've made a u-turn and went south on 41st. I can catch them if I can get us to Morrison as they are coming out to make the right back onto Market. Before I could hear ol' Thunder Cat roar again, my partner slapped his palms on top of the dashboard and got on his high horse again.

"Look, man. I know why we are here ut's to nail that murderer Tiny Blue Rocc but I have a thirteen year old daughter at home and I can't allow those hoodlums down there to continue. One of those fuckers just slapped her! So, if you're not driving down there so we can stop that..." His arm flew in front of my face, his finger was erect and pointing straight at the commotion in the middle of the street.

"Then I will run my ass down there and stop it myself."

Deshaun

Chapter 29

It took every milligram of strength I had left to push myself onto my feet and grab Sky. Her back was perched against the concrete wall on the left side of the liquor store with a bloodied paper towel held to her mouth. I put my hand underneath her arm by her armpit and led her across the street with me, back towards my uncle's house. "We gotta get the fuck outta here, the Babylons are on their way."

My legs could hardly hold me up without wobbling. Holding Sky underneath her arm kept me from falling back down to the pavement. The wails of sirens over the hill were getting closer. Our pace quickened. "Let's go, Sky, hurry the fuck up!" No sooner than those instructions left my lips did the police come from each direction on 41st and trap us like mice in a maze. The way they cornered us, the nosey neighbors standing in their doorways must have thought we were the ones doing all the ass whooping.

A 1964 silver smoke gray Mustang was the lead horse of the black and white patrol cars that stopped twenty yards ahead of us. I pulled Sky's arm closer to me so her chest was pushed against mine, the plain-clothed officers were now sixty feet away from us. I wrapped my arms around her beaten body and spoke into the crest of her neck. "Don't say shit. You hear me?" I let Sky's body go and her puppy dog eyes regained their strength. She blotted her upper lip with the paper towel, pulled her shoulders back, and lifted her chin to match her posture.

Placing my trigger finger underneath Sky's chin, I forced her eyes to meet mine. "Remember, if they ask you what happened, the story is that someone ran up on us from behind and tried to rob us and we fought to keep our belongings. Remember, we have no idea what they look like, they had on ski masks and we didn't see any faces." Sky glanced at me, her lips slightly open and loose. Her eyes fixated on the red and blue lights jumping off the walls around us. Her confidence was slowly fading. I placed my palms over her exposed clavicle and gripped her shoulders. "You hear me? We don't know who it was. That's the story, so stick to it." She nodded her head like a child being reprimanded by her father.

In my peripheral I could see each set of uniform officers exit their squad cars and fan out to talk to the neighbor's, that were still standing in front of their houses. The two Detectives approaching us looked like they were undercover butt buddies with their matching handlebar mustaches that extended to their chin. The driver was only taller than his partner by what seemed like half a yard. They were both in wrangler blue jeans, button up shirts and sunshades but the driver wore his a little different. The sleeves of his red and black flannel were rolled up right above his elbows. The inside of his left arm, two inches north of his wrist, was a tattoo of a skeleton with red flames around its head, riding what looked like a Harley Davidson. His sun-beat skin made the lines etched around his mouth look like valleys compared to his babyface partners.

"Well, well, well. If it isn't Mr. Track Star himself. Looks like you couldn't sprint yourself away from that ass kicking, huh?" His pale face erupted in laughter and started to match the color of his flannel. Detective whatever his name was, had jokes and I damn sure wasn't in the mood to hear them, but it looks like I don't have much of a choice. I remember seeing that same tattoo hanging out of the Mustang when Pernell drew down on B Braze in the set over a month ago. He stared at my shoes and brought his attention back to my aching face. "So, what is your dumbass doing over here?"

Knowing I wasn't in the best position to get smart, I answered his question the same way I hoped Sky was doing ten feet away from me with his partner. "I came over here to hang out with my friend." I nodded in Sky's direction. "Is that a problem, Officer?"

He pointed at my face, then to a couple of blood droplets that landed on the edge of my sleeve on my white tee. "The way your face looks, it doesn't seem like you have any of those around here."

Detective Dipshit thought he was on a roll. I pointed at Sky as she was still getting questioned by his partner. He glanced at his partner then back at me. "Well listen up, we got a call that there was a group of dumb, black motherfuckers fighting in front of the liquor store. So you're telling me that wasn't you getting your ass whooped over there?"

I know he saw the road rash across my face because I felt it burning as the sun continued to beat on it, but I wasn't going to admit to anything. I kept my lips stitched. He nodded his head up and down, turned his back and spoke into his walkie-talkie. My adrenaline was wearing off and every punch and kick

I took to the body and head was starting to take its toll. He put his walkie-talkie back on his belt, pivoted and faced me. "Witnesses said it was a guy in blue jeans, a white shirt and red shoes fighting about four other guys." I didn't know what he thought he was going to get out of me but I wasn't going to say a word about it. He tossed out his fishing line, again, to see if I was going to bite. "Look kid, you're the victim. You're not in any trouble, just give me your side of how it all went down."

He pulled his pen out of his back pocket, opened his index card sized notepad, flipped to the middle and waited for my response. My heart almost jumped through my bird chest and landed at his boots. "Nah, that wasn't me, Officer."

My answer rubbed him the wrong way, his weathered face matched the red squares in his flannel and the muscle along his jaw line looked like it was on steroids. The words I was hearing come out his mouth fought their way through his clenched teeth but his jaw never moved again. "Look here, you dumb fuck. We already have witnesses saying they jumped you and your friend. All you need to do is let me know who it was so I can let you and your lady friend go."

The shorter detective, the one that was questioning Sky a minute ago, interrupted his partner questioning me. "Aye, Braveheart, come here. It looks like his lady friend has a little bit more sense than he does." Detective Braveheart made his way towards his partner.

Every second that passed a new thought of what Sky might have told the detectives rushed to the prefrontal cortex of my mind and started to play tricks on me. Detective Braveheart stepped himself into my circle of space and stuck his finger in the center of my sternum. "So, you really want us to believe that bullshit story she is over there telling my gullible ass partner?"

On the inside, the square me was clapping, screaming and jumping around but I remained under control physically. Sky did exactly what I wanted her to do, now it was my turn. I lifted my chin and matched the gaze of Detective Braveheart's. "What story are you talking about, officer, the truth?"

That question poked the sleeping bear. He threw his notebook at my chest and tossed his ballpoint pen across the street landing in what looked like a witness's front lawn. "You little fucking piece of shit…" Detective Braveheart closed his eyes, inhaled and leaned his face close to my ear. "Truthfully, I don't give a fuck what happened to you. I wish you dumb fucks would have killed each other. That would have been less paperwork for me."

"Fuck you," I whispered back. Detective Braveheart's eyes darted over my shoulder to see if the ladies standing in front of their homes were still watching us. He drew his arm around my neck like we were long lost pals and stuck me with a short concise hook to the soft spot of my stomach. I tried to reflate my lungs but I was suffocating. The tiny bit of air I had left was wheezing it's way out into the atmosphere.

Detective Braveheart walked towards his partner without looking back in my direction. My vision was blurry from the loss of oxygen but my ears still worked perfectly. "Whitehead, let's get the fuck out of here and let these fuckers purge themselves." Detective Whitehead whistled loud enough so the whole block could hear and made a lasso motion with his finger. The last set of uniform officers left the houses and hopped back into their patrol cars and vanished as fast as they appeared.

Sky quickly walked back to me and placed one hand on my lower back and her other hand where my heart was and tried pushing me back into a vertical position. She grabbed both my wrists and lifted my arms high above my head. "Look at me Deshaun, deep breath baby. Again, one more time." After about the sixth time I was able to let my arms down.

I pulled Sky as close as I could to my face. The dry tear lines that ran through her foundation on her cheeks looked like Cherokee war stripes on a beaten warrior. I took my thumb and ran it across her cheek. "What did you tell 'em Sky?"

Sky placed each of her hands on the sides of my face and looked me in my eyes, the white around her right pupil was filled with blood. "I told 'em exactly what you told me to tell 'em."

A small grin crawled across my swollen lips. I leaned in towards Sky's forehead and kissed the center of it. "What's that for?" she asked.

"Because you did everything I asked you to do, no questions asked." Her face lit up like a match in a dark room. The little girl inside her yearning for compliments gushed outwardly with admiration.

She pressed her lips against my swollen lips and wrapped her arm around my waist. "I'ma get you back to your uncle's house. I got you."

Chapter 30

It didn't matter how many times I closed my eyes and imagined different scenarios of what took place by the liquor store, or how many times I wrote what I could have done differently in my journal. The fact of the matter is, I'm lying in my bed with a pack of frozen peas placed on the side of the face and my body is sensitive to anything that touches it. If I would've kept my guard higher like Pernell showed me in P-Nutt's garage, maybe I wouldn't have gotten dope fiend. Maybe if I would've been the aggressor and kept my attention on one nigga and worked the dog shit out of him like Pernell did the *ese* at the trolley station, I could've come out with a better outcome. The more "ifs" I wrote down in my journal, the more I understood what needed to happen next.

Before I could reach the cordless phone, the familiar rhythmic taps came dancing across my window. Initially, I didn't want to tell Pernell anything that happened because I was afraid of what might have to happen again, and afraid of the nightmares that will accompany me in my sleep.

Pernell's voice penetrated the single pane glass window before I pushed myself off my bed to my feet. His voice had a little more bite to it this morning. "Getcha ass up, nigga, and meet me at the dungeon in twenty minutes. Don't be late ru!"

I got to the garage in under fifteen minutes. Pernell and Arm Hammer stood in the center only separated by Arm & Hammer's outstretched arm pointing in my direction. "Check it out, Y.A., on Piru, I ain't fucking with blood. Ain't no way on God's green earth I'm riding for this goofy ass nigga. On Piru, I ain't finna bust a grape for blood. The dumbass nigga shouldn't have been over there fuckin' wit that brosstown bitch anyways."

Pernell always tried convincing Arm & Hammer that I was bool, but it was something about me that he just didn't like. I could never figure it out, but it was starting to get annoying. Instead of me standing there listening I interjected my feelings before Pernell could stick up for me again. "Check it out A.H., I ain't come over here to ask you to do shit for a nigga. Pernell told me to come so I came. But truth be told, when I go handle what needs to be handled, you can sit cha black ass down somewhere. I don't need nothing from you my nigga." The part of me that was scared to speak up finally won the battle. D Hogg was emerging and he was skinning the layers of Deshaun off himself in front of everyone in the garage.

Arm & Hammer's rage held all the power of a wildfire, I could practically see the flames from his narrow nostrils. He was now only a foot away, his fist loosely balled. "What is you sayin' then, nigga?"

I stood there not saying another word. He knew exactly what I was saying without me having to say it. I was with however he wanted to handle this. Win, lose, or draw it didn't matter. I wasn't going to allow disrespect to continue any longer. I put the brew I picked up from the weight bench back down and jacked my jeans over my waist. Pernell quickly hopped in between us.

"Why the fuck you always savin' this square ass nigga for?" Arm & Hammer tried pushing Pernell out the way but he was solid as an oak. "You know what then ru," Arm & Hammer grabbed his pistol off the wooden table next to the cooler and stuffed it in his waist. "You two dumbass niggas handle that shit then. Pernell, since you vouchin' for blood you know what's hatnin'. Y'all niggas got twenty-fo. I'm gone ru!"

Chapter 31

—◄•◦•►—

Tonight there isn't a cloud in the sky that's going to cover me from God's watching eye. Pernell came back to the Dungeon with Krystal's Lexus and picked me up. The freeway had an eerie emptiness to it. The pieces of metal that congested the lanes during the day were now gone and the freedom of not being seen was scary.

Pernell hasn't said a word since we left the set but even if he did I wouldn't have heard a word. The only thing I could hear was Arm & Hammer's voice, the constant loop of it bouncing off the corners of my mind like the blue rubbery ball inside a racquetball court. Maybe Arm & Hammer was right, maybe I shouldn't have been fucking with Sky. Maybe if I didn't forget the condoms in my top drawer then maybe I wouldn't have gotten jumped at the liquor store. But none of that shit matters now, all that matters is I have twenty four hours.

Pernell kept the Lexus in the slow lane and didn't go one mile per hour over sixty five. He reached for the controller in the middle console and turned the volume down until it showed a blue three, then he finally spoke. "Check it out D, this is how we finna get brackin'. Once we exit Imperial, I'ma bang a left on 47th and park underneath the bridge. Boguard said his relative Tiara told him them niggas was finna be at the American Legion because one of them bitch ass niggas just got out or some shit. So that's where we finna go."

I knew exactly where the American Legion was, I went once three years ago with my dad to celebrate my uncle Juney's sixtieth birthday. I remember that day because it was the first time I heard my dad use any foul language towards my mom, ever. I've never seen my pops act like that before. There was something different in his eyes, something that was foreign to me but kin to my uncle. That night my dad traded his khaki slacks, white shirt and a tie for a pair of black jeans, a black shirt and a black leather jacket. His corporate vernacular was replaced with a city slicker's tongue. That was the first time I ever saw my dad, the real him, him before me.

Pernell slapped the steering wheel to get my attention. "Look nigga, once we park, all you have to do is walk a block up and the American Legion will be on your right. You're gonna have the first pick of the litter, my nigga. Make sure you knock a niggas noodles out."

My stomach was tying itself in knots and my fingers were doing the same. The .45 I placed under the seat when we left was now on my lap. I pulled the slide towards my chest and racked a bullet in the magazine well. From the corner of my eye I could see Pernell watching, studying my movements, studying to see if I was following all the protocols he showed me in P-Nutts garage. Those days of boxing just weren't boxing. Pernell taught me everything he knew and then some. The motto was if we stayed ready we wouldn't have to get ready.

Thirty Five yards away from the bridge Pernell nodded his head forward towards a Carolina blue Impala parked on a dirt lot across the street from the American Legion suspended in air. "That right there..." He paused. "That's their big homie Havoc's low-low. Blood just got out last month. P-Nutt said he did fifteen years in the feds for a string of bank licks that he and his potna's were hittin' from here to the bay. P-Nutt said the Impala used to be burgundy and it was his but he sold it to Havoc right before he got locked."

Pernell parked behind an RV that doubled as a smokers hangout. The veranda was pulled out as far as it could stretch, the factory shade was no longer attached and jumbo towels were hung down to the sidewalk taking its place. I tied the red bandana Pernell gave me two weeks earlier around the bottom half of my face, pulled the hoodie over my head and tightened the velcro on Franklins. All the reasons not to get out of the car came flooding in, as if my body sent a blanket invitation to accept what was done to me earlier. I took a deep breath, closed my eyes and let the thoughts pass through me before I asked God to cover me with his protection.

The warmth from the Santa Ana winds that had the sky half naked earlier were replaced with a noticeably sharp breeze sweeping in from the Pacific Ocean that sent the hairs on the back of my back neck to stand at attention. My pace matched the smokers that were aimlessly roaming the sidewalk. I didn't say a word to any of them. I kept walking, head down, listening for the voices from earlier.

A shopping cart with a tarp that was on its last days was bound to the fence in front of me. I took the .45 out from the waist of my jeans and crouched next to it and kept my ears open to the groups of conversations that were happening in the parking lot. I was only twenty-five yards away now and the voices were becoming clearer the quieter the beats of my heart became. Then a voice boomed across the parking lot. It was a tone that if you listened too long it would mesmerize you. Yet, it was powerful and commanding. "Aye, little homie, I heard about what you did today. That's how you clean up the set, cuz."

The next voice triggered my heart to stop and my ears to open up. "Don't even trip, cig homie, I love that type shit! Ain't no niggas finna get any passes when I'm around here. On the set, cuz!"

My grip tightened around the handle of the .45. That was him, the nigga who dope fiend me today and the nigga that slapped Sky. The butterflies in my stomach just had a million babies but I swallowed as many as I could while he kept running his mouth. "Give me fo' minutes I'm finna c right back, cuz. I'ma head to the car to grab some mo' drank and another blunt. I'm parked at the end of the fence."

I placed my forehead on my knees and rocked myself forward, copying the smokers next to me. A pair of blue Chuck Taylor's walked right by us, without giving us a second look. Raising my forehead from my knees the passenger door to a Ford Mustang was open and half of his body was inside of it looking for something. I jumped up from the shadows of the tent and ran to the car. "What's brackin', nigga? What's that Piru like?!"

His head turned to look at me, his eyes danced around trying to recognize my features behind my bandana. A devilish smirk appeared across his face when he recognized me. "Fuck you, cuz. You's a bitch!"

The .45 in my hand was pointed at the middle of C tattooed between his eyes. "No, fuck you, nigga!" Before another breath left his expiring soul, I squeezed the trigger.

Chapter 32

It doesn't matter how much water I allow to run over my head and down my body, the images from last night are stitched to the inside of my eyelids. Every time I blink I relive it again and again, the driblets of blood exploding from the quarter-size hole in his forehead finding their way onto my face. In the movies, the blood looks thin and watery like you can wipe it away with the back of your hand and it'll vanish, but that wasn't the case. It was cemented in my eyebrows, and glued to my forehead like snot on a rag. I thought killing somebody last night was somehow going to magically make me feel better but it really didn't make me feel anything. The emptiness was still here. It's like a void. A dark void. A never-ending void.

Three rapid knocks against the bathroom door caught my attention and pulled me out of my own black hole. My mom slid her arm through the crack of the door and placed the cordless phone on the counter next to my toothbrush. Even with a hint of sarcasm, my mom's voice sounded better than the one that kept talking in my head. Her words bounced off the steam filled mirror. "Deshaun, if you don't get your ass out my shower and quit wasting all that damn water. You have a phone call. Some girl named Sky is asking for you." My mom's arm slid back through the door and I was once again left alone in my own thoughts.

I turned the spout clockwise until the water dried up. What could Sky want? She can't already want to hang out again? I pulled the Star Wars towel from the towel rack that my mom bought from Disney World as a souvenir, dried my body then wiped the steam from the mirror. I picked up the phone and placed it on my ear. "Hello."

"Where the fuck were you last night, Deshaun?"

Sky's questioning caught me off guard but I recovered well. "I was at the pad with my mom. She had me watching Steel Magnolias with her for the hundredth time. Why, what's up?"

"Deshaun, don't play dumb with me. You know why."

Sky was right I did know why but I damn sure wasn't going to tell on myself and tell her. Rule number three was to never tell anyone any of your business because you never know, one day they could start to hate you and then become an eye witness. I kept silent hoping she would change the subject but she didn't.

"So you're telling me that wasn't you last night who shot Tiny Awol?"

I knew the question was coming but my words left me. I couldn't will my lips to move. My mind went blank and my eyes widened as I stared at myself in the mirror. Sky didn't want to know the truth, she didn't want to know the nightmare I lived out last night. She is only concerned with her own conscience, if she was part of the blame why another young black male had to die.

I stared at the monster I was becoming in the mirror. D Hogg was emerging and Deshaun was evaporating like the steam on the bathroom mirror. The kid who dreamt of playing college football like his dad and earning an engineering degree was as dead as Tiny Awol. There was no turning back into the innocent kid that used to sneak tokes of weed from Alex's sister's bong, and had weekend sleepovers at Lee's to watch Star Trek marathons. Those days, even though they were only months ago, are long gone.

I held the phone in front of my mouth like it was a microphone and spoke clearly. "Nah, that wasn't me who shot that nigga; but you know how the sayin' goes… life's a bitch and then you die."

Sky gasped at my coldness. Her emotions leaped through the phone and snugged at a piece of my heart that was still there but it wasn't enough to change the facts. The fact was, them niggas jumped me and they had what was comin'. The bitch ass nigga Tiny Awol knew what the fuck was gonna happen, it's an eye for an eye, that's the rules. "That's fucked up, Deshaun. How could you? It was only a fight. You and I might have some bumps and bruises but we're still alive. Why do you niggas do this? I just don't get it."

I wondered how she could fix her mouth and say that to me when she was right there and witnessed how they did me, but I couldn't allow my anger to cause me to say the wrong thing and indict myself over this phone. "Check it out Sky, it wasn't me. Ok? But karma's a bitch. I guess I wasn't the only nigga he dope fiend before."

Sky's voice went quiet for a second. Maybe she was believing the story I was giving her or maybe she wasn't but I was starting to care less and less about what she had to say. "Is this why you called me this morning, Sky? To ask me questions behind some bitch ass nigga who's dead in his car?"

"No, Deshaun. That's not why I called. I'm sorry for asking. I really wanted to make sure you were ok… that's all."

I could appreciate Sky's concern, but it was none of her business what happened last night. She only needed to know what I wanted to tell her, and I wasn't telling her shit. Sky finally changed the subject. "The real reason I called you was to invite you to this bonfire my homegirls and I are having for Labor Day Weekend. We do one every year and I want you to come and hang out with me."

I glanced at the wall above my dresser looking for a calendar. "When is that?"

Sky placed her tongue on the roof of her mouth and sucked. "That's this Saturday, stupid."

She paused and waited for me to answer. It sounded like a great idea, but I needed to know who was going to be there, especially knowing everything that transpired. I trust Sky but not her homegirls. "Look, Sky. I wanna come but I need to know who's gonna be there besides me, you and your homegirls. Because if they're gonna have a bunch of random niggas there, I'm-"

Sky cut me off. "Deshaun, they're not. I promise. The only random nigga that's finna be there is you." Sky laughed at her own joke. "It's just gonna be me and my homegirls there and that's it."

How can I say no and pass up being around Sky, I can't do that. Maybe we can finish what we started at my uncle's house. "Ok, I'm in but I'm gonna bring a couple of my friends to occupy yours. What time should I show up?"

"I don't know yet, but I will call you when I do, promise."

As she was about to hang up I got her attention. "Sky, just want to thank you for checkin' up on me. I appreciate you actin' like you really care about a nigga."

Sky giggled and her voice brought a smile to my face. "Deshaun, I do care and that's why I'm thanking you for riding for us."

Tiny Blue Rocc

Chapter 33

I got a call from Cowboy the same time I was pulling my shirt over my head trying to creep out of Vanessa's bedroom before she woke up. His voice was colder than the receiver that was pressed against the side of my face. The shit I was hearing I didn't want to believe. How could the homies let Tiny Awol get caught slippin' in his own whip while they were partying inside the American Legion for Havoc's homecoming? None of that shit made any fuccin' sense to me. The crazy part was, I saw cuz less than twenty-four hours ago. I just watched him and his squad beat the brakes off of Juney's square ass nephew Deshaun in front of the liquor store.

Cowboy said it happened around midnight but I was too busy stuffing Vanessa with this Crip dick to hear anything over her hollerin' ass. Come to think of it, I thought I heard something during our intermission but put it off as one of those M-1000's that those bad ass pepe's be lighting when they come back from TJ. But I was wrong, hella fuckin' wrong.

By the time I got to granny's house the first thing I did was wash Vanessa's juices off my face and dick.

There was no way in hell granny was finna let me eat some of her grits before I did that. She told me once before not to come into her house stankin', let alone her kitchen smelling like last night's trash and since that moment, I've never done it again. Once I got to Lil Blue Rocc's plot Cowboy was there waiting for me.

Delicately etched in front of Lil Blue Rocc's headstone was a detailed design of his government name spelled out horizontally across the grass with royal blue long stem roses. The picture Mrs. Jackson chose to be encrusted into his headstone was one I've never seen before and the smile on his face made me look away.

Cowboy stood next to me silent, pacing, waiting for me to say something but I was speechless. I picked off the shreds of grass that were stuck on the blue rag hanging over Lil Blue Rocc's headstone. The Crown Royal felt like acid the longer I held the bottle to my mouth but I could care less, it didn't matter what I was doing to myself, I was still alive to do whatever the fuck I wanted and my nigga wasn't. Cowboy finally broke the silence. "What's up wit all this quiet shit, nigga? Why the fuck do you got me here, cuz?"

The Crown Royal burnt my chest as I took another guzzle before I answered. "Cause, nigga. I know who set me and the homie up."

Cowboy stopped pacing, kneeled next to me and threw his cell phone far enough to his left so that it was out of ears reach. "Who told you, Vanessa?" I shook my head yes. "How do you know that bitch ain't lyin' to you, nigga? And plus, we already knocked the slob niggas brains back fo' that. What you need to be focusin' on is what just happened to Tiny Awol last night. 'Cause on the dead homies, you know the diru nigga they say smoked the homie so you need to be the nigga to handle that."

Cowboy was right, I needed to knock off Deshaun but I also needed to knock off one more person and I might be able to kill two birds with one stone with the information Vanessa handed over to me last night.

After I swiped her down her mouth became a flood gate. For her to claim that the Sky bitch was her "best friend" it sure didn't seem like it with all the information that was rushing outta her mouth. Vanessa told me she was in Sky's bedroom flat ironing her hair when she overheard Sky call B Braze to tell him that Lil Blue Rocc and I were on our way.

The best part of Vanessa running her fuccin' mouth was her telling me about the bonfire that her, the punk bitch Sky, and three other homegirls were having for Labor Day next Saturday alongside the Dana Point Hotel. She mentioned it was some sort of routine they do every year so they can turn up one last time before the summer ended. Little does she know it's going to be the last time any of them bitches turn up in life again.

Detective Braveheart

Chapter 34

The minute hand on my watch was a quarter past the twelve and still no fucking site of our C.I. It doesn't matter how much you pay these dumb motherfuckers, a nigger is always going to be a nigger, ain't no changing that. You would think me giving him two thousand dollars a month for his information would have him here on time but I guess I'm wrong. All I know is if we have to wait here another five minutes his dumbass will be in that welfare line waiting on a check like his mother.

His information is always good, never great, but what it's been doing is moving me up the ladder for the captain's seat when he leaves next year and with one more high profile conviction, I will be a shoo-in. Then I can finally find some free time to find a good woman. It's been close to three years now since Jenny left me. I thought if anyone understood what it was like to be a cop and love what they do it would've been her. I would've bet my house on it and I would've lost.

I met Jenny five years ago at a Gang Task Force Conference, I was asked to guest speak in Orange County. Jenny, at that time, was the Lieutenant at the

Harbor Division Gang Task Unit, and up until that day, I've never met a woman who saw the problem of gang violence the way I did. Her philosophy was like mine. If you want to be a gang member, then you want to go to jail and we will gladly be the ones to put you there. That's what I loved about her, she was a firecracker and it wasn't because of her red hair that hung to the middle of her shoulder blades, it was because she didn't take shit from anyone, not even me. We were one in the same. So when I got her letter the day before we were supposed to meet at LAX to fly to Puerto Rico to celebrate our two year anniversary, it threw me off.

Dear Honey Bear,

I'm not sure how to start this letter but I feel like we need to talk. I've been thinking about us a lot lately. Things used to be so great - it was like we were made for each other. I never thought I could love again after my husband was murdered but you showed me otherwise. I mean, everyone said it was perfect. I thought we would be together forever but things change and I don't see how this is going to work any longer.

A relationship is about spending time with one another and now that I've been promoted to Captain and you are on the fast track to your promotion, our time, the little bit that we have now, will be erased. What drew us together is what looks like is now pushing us apart and I don't want you to resent me later for not giving you my all.

I'm sorry. I wish I didn't have to do this, this way, but I couldn't see myself looking into those huge puppy dog eyes of yours and being strong enough to tell you this. I LOVE YOU Ray-Nathan Braveheart and if it's God's will, then we'll find our way back to each other. Until we meet again.

Love Jenny

Jenny's letter was a slap in the face. I couldn't see how she said spending time together was going to be more of a problem. I gave her every spare minute I had left. I know there weren't many but what else did she expect. What she didn't know was I was going to surprise her with the news that I was planning on transferring to Orange County so we could be closer and spend more time together, but she ruined that.

My partner's voice broke up the nightmare I was torturing myself with and his arm was outstretched over the dashboard pointing at the bathrooms at our one o'clock. "Aye Ray, do you see that?"

Our C.I. wasn't by himself and that was rule number fucking one; don't bring or tell anyone. I don't give a fuck if he was with Jesus himself, the rule was to be alone. I didn't need another nigger with their hand out looking for me to save them. Plus this is off the books. I'm paying this fucker with the money out of my own pocket.

I nodded to my partner and gave him the look. He knew what to do. We've been together thirty-six months now so he knew the procedure. Follow me. Get to the target. Watch my back. Secure the scene.

With my left hand, I pointed at my eyes then at the bathroom entrance. We don't need to get caught with our pants down regardless of how many times we meet. You can never trust a monkey farther than you can throw them and I stopped lifting weights years ago.

The bathroom looked empty at first glance, no one by the two sinks or the urinal, but underneath the stall doors was a set of black Nike's and a pair of white Chuck Taylor's with red shoe strings. Raising my 9 at the stall door, I looked to my partner and mouthed on the count of three. "One, two…" Before I got to three the door swung open. "Both of you, hands the fuck up!"

The two faces looked at me and didn't blink an eye. Our C.I. stood in front of his friend and smiled. His teeth and pupils were the only color I saw on his black face. He held a cigar filled with marijuana and blew a cloud in my direction. "Calm down top flight. Ain't no one finna do shit to y'all. Remember, you hate them as much as I love my money. I'm not gonna fuck that off. If I don't snitch, I don't eat."

Our C.I. laughed but what he didn't know was that I didn't give a fuck if he ate or not. I just wanted his information. He could die tomorrow for all I fucking cared. Truth be told, I hated a motherfucker who snitched on their own people and then swore to be loyal to me, like I was really going to trust them. To me, they are the filthiest pieces of shit on the face of the planet. None of them can fully be trusted, everything they do and say favors their own self-interest.

Before I could ask him anything, his mouth opened and information started spilling out. The shit that was coming out of his mouth didn't mean shit to me. I didn't care who was selling meth to soccer moms or which "OG" was pimping on some young girl. I only wanted to know who in the fuck was in my city pulling all the triggers and dropping these niggers like flies. I want murder convictions, that's it.

My partner had enough of the frivolous talk and unhooked his cuffs from his belt and snatched our C.I.'s malnourished wrist and slammed him against the wall. "Is this what you think my partner and I came out here for? Do you think we really care about any of the bullshit you just told us? The only reason why we are here is because you called my partner and told him that you knew who shot Tiny Awol."

Wrestling his wrist away he spun around and pointed to his right. "Why do you think they're here?"

The information we heard next was exactly what we needed to hear. They were able to tell the time it went down, the color of the car and what type of gun was used. It was the missing piece to the puzzle but I didn't want my dick to get too hard over the news because I knew how this type of information plays out in court. It's all hearsay from a non credible source and any seasoned public defender can get this type of information thrown out in preliminaries. In order for us to get this evidence to stick, we need some sort of acknowledgment of the murder from the suspect with some intimate details of the crime scene. And we need it on tape.

Jonas Royster

I holstered my gun and looked at our C.I.'s friend square in the eyes. It was my turn to play the good cop for once. I removed any emotion from my voice and spoke slow enough so they could understand every syllable. "Since you said the suspects are always at your house we are going to need you to wire up."

Before I could complete another thought I was interrupted. "Ain't no one wearin' a muthafuckin' wire. What the fuck are you tryin' to do, get me killed?"

"Calm down man. If you would've let me finish then you would know I'm not talking about physically wearing one but putting one in your house. All it is, is a tiny circular microphone that's no bigger than a watch battery. It picks up conversations thirty-five feet away, all you have to do is stick it to the back of your TV in your living room. The device has four undetectable microphones built-in so it picks up every sound in the room and it's always recording."

Our new friend examined the microphone recorder in the palm of my hand. "You sure no one will find out?"

A smile the size of my grandfather's plantation back in Mississippi spread across my face. "I'm sure of it. All you have to do is set it down and turn it on. We'll be listening on the other end. You don't have a thing to worry about, we'll handle the rest. I promise."

Deshaun

Chapter 35

Day 91:

I haven't written much because I'm scared of what will end up on paper. The last sixty-four days have felt like an accelerated course on how to become a young gangsta. I've learned how to steal, knock a muthafucka out, and now how to go on a mission and get my first K. This time last summer Lee and I were studying for SAT's in the Mediterranean garden next to Hepner Hall at SDSU. There's no way on God's green earth I would've guessed my whole life would be flipped on its head just a year later.

How in the fuck did I go from planning to go to college to planning an alibi for what I did to Tiny Awol the other night? It's my dad's fault. That's how. If he would've just kept his promise to my mom and I, then I would've never been uprooted from my dream. Now that dream is gone, just like my relationship with him. It was all a fucking mirage. I'm in a jungle where it's eat or be eaten, and I'm only hungry enough not to die.

Watching Tiny Awol's brains being blown across his headrest still hasn't stopped replaying in my mind.

It's like an NFL replay on a continuous slow-motion loop. Whenever I shut my eyes longer than a minute it would appear. The Valium I've been stealing from the prescription bottles my mom hides in her bra drawer have been helping me sleep, but when I'm awake, I can't seem to shake the images.

I wish Pernell would've told me that day at the park that nothing in my life was ever going to be the same. If he would've only chopped it up with me the night before and gave me the whole rundown, on how the nightmares slowly start to eat away at your sanity and how paranoia starts becoming your best friend. If what I read is true, that "total paranoia is total awareness," then what do I need to be aware of?

Chapter 36

A fter not getting a response from knocking on Pernell's door I knew to go back in the house and call Krystal's house. Over the last two months, Pernell was spending more time at Krystal's house as she was getting closer to her due date. Pernell said Krystal was having a hard time with the pregnancy, and he wanted to be there as much as possible.

The phone only rang once before I heard his voice. Pernell was his carefree self, his voice as smooth as the other side of the pillow. He spoke like there wasn't a worry in the world, like what I did to Tiny Awol last weekend didn't even bother him. "D, what's brackin' my nigga? I ain't heard from you since you did your thang last weekend. You bool?"

No shit he hasn't heard from me, he told me to stay my high yellow ass in the house and out the way. In the background I could hear Boguard and Arm & Hammer arguing over if the Oregon player had control of the football as he crossed the plane of the endzone. I waited a minute for the commotion to die down before I answered Pernell. "Yea, I'm bool. I'm hittin' you because I wan-"

"D, look. I gotta get off this phone. These niggas is finna chunk'em behind this dumb ass game. Just slide through ru. We can chop it up when you get here."

By the time I made it to Krystal's apartments I felt like I went through an urban obstacle course. The routine path of me walking straight down Alta View until I got to the liquor store, then crossing the street to Krystal's apartments on the right, has now become ten times more strategic. I didn't need to be seen by anyone, especially by those two dumbass GSU detectives that jacked me up after I got jumped last week.

I had to hop the security gate to the apartments next to ours so I wouldn't have to walk down the main street to get to Krystal's apartments. Taking that route added another ten minutes to my walk but it was worth my safety. Walking up the flight of stairs to Krystal's apartment had me fantasizing about one day getting Sky pregnant. Having a baby with her would be like hitting the lottery for me.

Pernell must've heard me stomping my way up the flight of stairs because the door was already open by the time I reached the top. When I walked through the door, the homies' faces lit up. They seemed extra excited to see me today. Even A.H. seemed to be a bit happy to see me.

"What's brackin', my nigga?" Boguard said, with a smile on his face that reached from ear to ear. He stood up from the couch to give me the P. "I've been outta town for a little bit and now all of a sudden you're brackin' like that?!"

I looked at Pernell, confused. I could've sworn he said don't tell a fucking soul, not even the homies. Not knowing if this was a test or not, I stuck to the script and kept quiet.

Pernell chimed in since my mouth was still shut. "D Hogg, quit actin' like that. You know I had to tell the homies that was us."

I grabbed a Karl Strauss Red Trolley off the coffee table and took a swallow. "Nah my nigga, I still don't know whatchu niggas are talkin' about." I said with a devilish grin.

Boguard looked at me and then back at Pernell. I noticed the confusion in his eyes. "Say no more, I get it ru. But for the record, you're bick for that one, D Hogg."

Any lingering doubt about what I did last weekend was being washed away by the homie's praise. Pernell once again looked like he didn't have a worry in the world but he could tell there was still something bothering me. "Why you trippin', D? It's been a week now, we're good."

I looked at Pernell square in his eyes so he could feel the words that were about to come out of my mouth. "I ain't trippin', my nigga. I just don't need everyone knowin' my fuckin' business. You told me before the less niggas who know, the less who can tell."

Pernell placed his hand on top of my right shoulder, like a teacher talking to a student. "I get it, D, but I had to let some of the homies know what happened. I didn't want to leave the homie's blind around the set." Pernell was right. I never looked at it from that perspective. If they didn't know what happened then they couldn't be on their p's and q's and if something happened to them then that would fall on me. Pernell continued. "I didn't give these niggas any details. I just let 'em know we up one, and you scored." Pernell's smile widened.

217

"I get it but keep that shit low though. The fewer homies that know, the better. As you said, a muthafucka can't tell what he doesn't know."

Pernell lit the blunt that was behind his ear before he spoke. "Don't worry my nigga, I got chu." Pernell shot me the P and passed me the blunt. "When you called me, it sounded like you was finna tell me somethin'. What's hatnin'?"

I sat on the barstool next to the kitchen. "I was hittin' you to see if you wanted to smash to this bonfire."

"Who's throwin' it?"

"My little cha-cha."

Pernell laughed. "Who the fuck is that nigga?"

"Baby I was with when I got jumped; Sky."

Pernell raised his eyebrow but Arm & Hammer's voice was the one I heard first. "Hell no, nigga, is you brazy? Ain't that the bitch that got all this shit brackin'?" Arm & Hammer made his way towards me from the living room. "And, word has it, she was the one who set up Lil Blue Rocc nigga, and his homie."

What Arm & Hammer was saying was news to me but at the end of the day, I didn't care. She didn't set me up or snitch on me. She was right there with me at that liquor store and even got her face slapped trying to help me. I took another swig from my beer before I answered. "Look A.H., I don't know anything about the Lil Blue Rocc shit, and gettin' jumped at the liquor wasn't her fault."

Arm & Hammer slapped his hand on the kitchen counter. "I know you don't know, nigga, that's why I'm tellin' you. You don't even know the type of bitch you're fuckin' wit, brazy-ass nigga.

Boguard walked over to the refrigerator and took out some cranberry juice to mix with his vodka. "Both y'all niggas need to bick it. If the bitch was foul, she woulda been had blood brossed up by now."

Arm & Hammer waved his hand at Boguard's remarks and at my nonchalant attitude about Sky and went back to watching the USC Oregon game. I've been over Arm & Hammer's hating ass attitude for the last couple months now. It didn't matter what I did or said, he always had something to say about it. I tried reasoning with Pernell. "Look, I ain't worried about what blood talkin' about. Baby said she finna have like four or five homegirls and she wanted me to slide through with some homies." I looked over the room. "So, is you niggas comin' or what?"

The word homegirls got Boguard's attention instantly. He downed his drink and threw his plastic cup in the trash. Anytime there was an opportunity for him to be around some women he was all in. "D, did I just hear you say four or five homegirls?" I laughed and nodded my head. "Well nigga, you should've said that as soon as you walked in the house. Fuck what them niggas is talkin' about, I'm smashin' with you."

Pernell looked at the two of us like we lost our rabbit-ass minds. "You niggas is brazy. The bitch could be playin' both sides of the fence for all you know."

I didn't expect to hear that from Pernell. He knew how much I liked Sky. I've called him a handful of times asking him what I should do next and never once did he tell me not to fuck with her, so I don't understand why now. Pernell had a good girl on his side and I just wanted the same. "Look Y.A., you know I've been knowin' Sky for some years now, if she was actin' funny, she would've left me for dead when I got jumped."

Pernell took another swig of his Red Trolley and swished it around his mouth. He was taking his time before he answered. "A.H.?"

A.H. looked up from the game. "What's brackin' nigga? Can't you b I'm watchin' this shit?"

Pernell grabbed the remote from the glass dining room table and turned the TV off. "I need you to smash with these niggas, just in case somethin' does pop off."

I tried arguing with Pernell, that it wasn't that type of situation, that Sky wasn't that type of broad but he brushed my comments off to the side and looked me square in my face. "You know how we get down, nigga. There always has to be at least two shooters wherever we go."

Arm & Hammer's head started swaying from left to right before he jumped out of the recliner and pivoted one hundred and eighty degrees to face Pernell. "I ain't feelin' none of this gay ass shit! On Piru, this shit is stupid as fuck. It's funky right now and you niggas wanna go post up with some brosstown bitches!" A.H. pulled out his .40 cal and slammed it on the beat-up coffee table in front of the TV. "None of you dumb ass niggas got one of these but you wanna go out in the war!"

Pernell knew exactly what A.H. was going to say, because as soon as he slammed his pistol on the coffee table, Pernell handed me the .45 from last week. "Here you go, ru. I cleaned 'em up and put some fresh hollows in the clip."

I looked at the .45 in disbelief. "I thought you said you were gonna get rid of this?"

Pernell stuffed it in my hand. "Well I didn't, nigga, so take this for right now. You know what to do with it." I tucked the pistol underneath my shirt and didn't say another word. "Check it out, y'all niggas can take my BM's whip. We ain't finna do shit but watch some movies and lay up. Make sure you niggas don't spill no drank in her shit tho'."

Pernell tossed Arm & Hammer the keys but he swatted them away like an annoying mosquito. "I ain't nobody's chauffeur! Let one of them dumb ass niggas drive."

Boguard picked up the keys to the Lexus off the carpet and slid them in his back pocket. "I'll drive then, don't trip my nigga. Let's p-up."

Chapter 37

W ith all the huffing and puffing coming from the seat behind me I almost swore Arm & Hammer was some sort of fucking dragon. Ever since I met him that day at the park near the apartments, when he knocked out Buster Rob, he never seemed to like me. I don't know what I did or said to him but I was over giving a fuck about his shitty ass attitude.

The only time the nigga seems to be happy is when it's time for something to go down. Arm & Hammer was off like that so that's why I was surprised he was complaining when Pernell told him to come with Boguard and myself to the bonfire. If he was going to be doing all that sucking his teeth shit and talking out the side of his neck, he should've stayed his Oscar the Grouch ass back at Krystal's house with Pernell. At the end of the day, I know how to handle myself now. I don't need a fucking babysitter.

Boguard on the other hand wouldn't stop talking. These were the most words I've ever heard him say. Ever since P-Nutt socked him in the chest that day for not participating in the melee at the beach, that "I'm so gangsta" extraness was no longer visible. Whether or not that act was a facade I can't actually say but what I can say is I like this version better. He even cracked a couple of jokes about how he pushed up on me that day at the park and how we got down. Now mind you his version was way different than how I remember but that wasn't the point, he was now like another brother I always wished I had.

Boguard slid the green-leafed blunt out from the Tiffany blue plastic test tube and sparked it as he exited the loop on West Mission Bay then turned to look at me. The smile that was there a minute ago as he talked about our first encounter was replaced with a furrowed brow and an emotionless stare. "So, D Hogg, you really ain't finna tell a nigga?"

Boguard's question caught me off guard. Tell him about what? I already told him that Sky was going to have a few homegirls at the bonfire and that they should all be as fine as her. What else does he want me to tell him?

Boguard took another hit from the Garcia Vega before he passed it across the middle console towards me. His cough blended in perfectly with the Luni Coleone blaring from the two twelve JBL's in the trunk. "D, quit playin' stupid, you know what the fuck

I'm askin'. I'm talkin' 'bout how you smoked that bitch ass brab nigga who jumped you last weekend."

Boguard's pearly whites were the only thing I saw on his shadowy face. The white bridge of teeth seemed to run from ear to ear. His eyes kept darting from the road back to me as I inhaled the sweet kush aroma into my chest. I let the smoke stay in my lungs for another thirty seconds while I thought about what I was going to say. "Boguard, my nigga, I don't know what the homie done told you or what you've heard but I ain't did shit last weekend."

Boguard looked at me like I had shit on my face. The comradery we just built was dissolved that quick. He snatched the Garcia Vega from my hand and cut his eye as he made a right and quick left into the parking lot of the Dana Hotel. A hundred yards ahead of us was a confetti of fire being thrown in the sky by the ocean breeze. The flames from the bonfire pit danced alongside the silhouettes that stood next to them but there was one that stood out amongst the rest. It was a coke bottle shape that stood off to the right, away from the others. I remember holding that bottle at my Uncle Juney's house a couple weeks back. It was Sky and my eyes wouldn't let me blink if I wanted to.

Boguard parked the Lexus in the parking spot directly in between the two palm trees that framed the scene like a postcard. Sky was only twenty yards ahead of me and this time there was something different about her, something that connected us more than the lust that was starting to swirl in my pants. It was something more primitive, an aching kinship of protection. Doing what I did to Tiny Awol last week wasn't just solely about me and my manhood. It was also me secretly wanting to get some get-back for what they did to Sky that day as well.

The fire raging from the burning pallets behind Sky was just enough light for me to see the corner of her mouth curling up toward the moon. Her hips slowed their swaying and fell in rhythm with my stride. It took every drop of willpower I had in me not to run towards Sky and swallow her with a massive hug and drawn out kiss, as I saw in countless melodramatic movies with my mom.

I was now only eight yards away and Sky and her willpower broke before mine. She kicked off her sandals and sprinted at me and jumped on my lanky body like a spider monkey hugging a tree. Her tender kisses felt like tiny drops of water against my cheeks. From the corner of my eye, I noticed Boguard taking inventory of Sky's ass sitting firmly in my palms. "Damn, my nigga. It sure looks like someone is happy to see you."

Sky nibbled her lips along the crest of my neck up to my ear and gripped the edge of my ear with her teeth before she unwrapped her legs from my waist and slid off of me. I couldn't help but admire the beauty standing in front of me. Her white denim shorts looked like they were painted onto her skin, which hardly covered the bottom half of her ass but I wasn't complaining. If it wasn't for the .45 tucked in my waist, Sky would've felt that my dick was as hard as that metal.

Sky took my hands in hers and led me closer to the bonfire where the rest of her friends were. "Deshaun, I want you to meet my homegirls. These bitches right here ain't never switched up on me, not even when we were in seventh grade and the whole school was hatin' on me because I had every boy and their teachers jockin' me."

Sky's friends were as bad as she was. All three of them could have been in someone's music video but the one they called Vee, was giving Sky a run for her money. Her cocoa butter skin looked like it was sprinkled with gold glitter and her pixie layered hair made her a spitting image of Halle Berry in the movie Boomerang. And maybe I was staring too hard because I noticed Sky cutting an eye at me as I was looking over her friends.

Boguard didn't need an invitation to talk to any of Sky's friends. He was already mixing and mingling by the time Sky led me over there. Sky was watching Boguards every move like a mother hen watching her chicks. She told me not to bring any homies to the bonfire that were going to act thirsty, but with the fine-ass friends she has, I think any man in his right mind would be acting thirsty.

Sky got tired of watching Boguard sweet talk to her friends and rolled her eyes at me. All I could do was shrug my shoulders and smile. What did she expect? Her friends are bad as fuck and if I didn't have my eyes set on Sky, I would be doing exactly what Boguard was doing.

Sky shrugged off my smile and nodded her head towards the skeleton looking palm tree behind me. Arm & Hammer was alone. His back leaned against the palm tree with his right hand tucked underneath his hooded sweater, as he looked over each shoulder like he was in fucking Vietnam or something. "What's up with your weird-ass homie over there? Why is he actin' paranoid around a bunch of females? That nigga is on some weirdo shit."

Sky was right, Arm & Hammer looked like every bit of a weirdo right now. Other than going to the Puerto Rican Festival with him and Pernell, I've never been around Arm & Hammer outside the set. I remember being on the trolley with Pernell on our way to Horton Plaza Mall and he told me not to mind Arm & Hammer and his militant ways because ever since he had returned home from doing five in YTS, he had never really been the same.

Sky took my hand in hers and rubbed the inner part of her thumbs gently over the middle of my fingers. Her skin felt like the egyptian cotton my mom purchased when we visited Morocco three winters ago. Her almond shaped eyes moved away from Arm & Hammer and made their way back to me. I wrapped my hands around her waist and pulled her close enough to me that I could feel her nipples pressing against my chest.

Sky's beauty was different, her curves of softness were a perfect contrast to her tough girl persona. Her emotions were never easily hidden on her face and that was evident in the crease of her brow. She placed her left hand over my chest and spoke quietly into my ear. "Deshaun, I never really got to thank you for what you did for us." Sky lifted her eyes to meet mine. Her green eyes tonight were a shade that was hard to describe. It was almost like they were both green and yellow at the same time. I tried turning my head so I wouldn't get caught up in her beauty but there was some sort of an invisible force holding my face in place. "With all the niggas I done hung out with, none of them ever did what you did for me. Even when we got sweated by the police you gamed me up and knew what to say. Thank you, boo. Thank you for-"

I placed my finger over Sky's lips. There was no need for her to say the rest, I knew what she was going to say and I didn't need another reminder about it. I squeezed my arms tighter around her waist and she closed her eyes in anticipation of what was coming next.

I closed mine to match hers. Not caring if Boguard or Arm & Hammer saw me looking soft, I pressed my lips onto hers. Sky's lips were what I imagined a cloud would feel like. Soft and spongy but warm like a fleece blanket. Sky wrapped her wrists behind my neck and drew me into her. Her warm breath tickled my ear as she spoke. "I just want you to know Deshaun, I'm only fuckin' with you. I want to be your ride or die bitch."

Sky's body melted into my arms. The heat behind her sun-kissed skin made my dick start to stand at attention again. My nose noticed a scent of coconut escaping from Sky's skin and I buried my face in her neck searching for it. My lips moved slowly along her neck and down to her shoulder.

Her nipples were hardening against my chest as she cupped her petite hands along my face so we could look each other in the eyes. She inched her face closer to mine and initiated our second kiss, then I heard the gunshots. Four distant pops that didn't sound like much of anything at first. I wasn't even sure which direction the shots had come from.

Sky whispered, "Deshaun," and then she got quiet and very still. I couldn't tell if she was still breathing.

Before I realized what was happening, Sky slid through my arms. Her eyes widened with terror. Her whisper fell in the sand with her. Her arm tried to stretch out for me to lift her up but it didn't go any higher than her body.

That's when the pops turned into a barrage of shots and I fell into the sand next to Sky. We were both pinned behind the concrete wall of the bonfire pit and the bullets were chipping away at its protection. I inched forward on my stomach, so I could see around the retaining wall. I yelled over the high pitch screams that were penetrating my ears. "They're over by the bridge to our left, about a hundred yards out!"

I pointed to the flashing lights off in the distance hoping Arm & Hammer could get their exact location and start to shoot back. I knew I couldn't stay where I was any longer, the concrete wall in front of me was crumbling from all the gunfire. I had to make my move to the Lexus before I became a victim of multiple gunshot wounds to the body.

With one last look at flares illuminating from the muzzles in the distance I stood up and made a beeline to the car. Arm & Hammer saw my movement and unloaded his clip at the flashes in the darkness. As I positioned myself behind the passenger door of the Lexus I steadied my hand on the roof, closed my left eye to get a better aim on the flashes and began pulling the trigger of the .45, like I was strumming an electric guitar. The shell casings that were being ejected onto the roof sounded like the cymbals to a heavy metal band.

Then, before I could pull the trigger again, everything stopped and I couldn't hear a thing but the blaring ringing noise in my ears. All movement in front of me had paused and my ears were starting to regain their hearing again, but there was nothing to hear, it was quiet. There was an eerie silence that covered the mayhem that was laid out in front of me.

Arm & Hammer's voice broke the silence. "Is you niggas bool?!"

I ran my hand across my body to make sure I wasn't hit but the wetness in my hand stopped me. It was blood but it wasn't mine. I swallowed the lump in my throat and answered. "I'm good my nigga."

"Boguard, what about you?" Arm & Hammer asked, making sure we were all ok.

I couldn't hear Boguard's response because I was fixated on Sky's body that I left by the bonfire pit. I ran over to where she laid and tried to scoop her up. Her eyes were still open, but the life behind them was gone. There was no more of that playful fire dancing behind her pupils. That subdued pain that was always trying to jump out from behind her eyes was gone as well. Everything was gone now. Her lips were still pursed together as if she had one more whisper to tell me. The entry wound on her back was no bigger than a softball and her blood was starting to stain the sand.

The squeals from Sky's friends were deafening. The one she called Vee was standing over me yelling and hitting me on my back. I could feel her tears dripping on the back of my neck as I tried to wake up Sky. When I looked over to my right, I saw Arm & Hammer doing the same thing to Boguard's body that I'm doing to Sky's.

I ran over to Boguards body and tried to drag him out of the bonfire pit he was laying in but he wouldn't budge. Arm & Hammer grabbed me by the collar and dragged me off Boguard's body. "We gotta get the fuck up outta here. Let's go nigga! He's dead, D!"

I kept trying to pick up Boguard but his weight wouldn't allow me. I looked up for Arm & Hammer's help. "We just can't leave him like this. We gotta get him to a hospital. Him and Sky."

"D Hogg, we gots to go now! The homie and that faggot ass bitch of yours is dead. We stay any longer, we all finna go to jail."

Arm & Hammer was starting to sound like a broken record, but I knew he was right. There was nothing else I could do for Boguard or Sky. I let go of Boguards body and ran over to Sky and kissed her right above her eyes in the middle of her forehead. "I'm sorry, Sky."

By the time I hopped in the Lexus, Arm & Hammer was already on his cell phone talking to Pernell.

"Blood, we en route. They smoked Boguard!"

Chapter 38

——◆◆◆——

"What the fuck happened, nigga?!"

I stared at Pernell in disbelief. I didn't know what to tell him. I kept shaking my head like an Etch A Sketch hoping the images would magically erase somehow because I couldn't process the shit myself. One minute I was holding the girl who was going to carry my future first born son, then the next she was taken from me like sand slipping through my hands. To make matters worse, I got Boguard killed as well.

Arm & Hammer jumped in front of Pernell and in my face. "Quit shakin' your head, dumb ass nigga. You know what the fuck happened!" His finger was inches from my nose as he turned to look at Pernell. "This bitch ass nigga got the homie smoked!"

Arm & Hammer's fist whizzed past my chin. There wasn't much room in Krystal's one bedroom apartment but I got enough space between Arm & Hammer and I that I was able to square him off. This has been a long time coming. This wasn't about Boguard at all; this was about the fact that Arm & Hammer never liked me. He never believed that a nigga that wasn't born and raised in the set should be from it.

Pernell stepped in between us. "Y'all niggas gotta bick it. This ain't the time for us to be at each other's necks." Pernell walked Arm & Hammer towards the sliding glass door that led to a teeny balcony overlooking the courtyard of the apartments. "Do any of you niggas know who the fuck it was?"

I paused to let Pernell's question sink in. I didn't see shit. As soon as I heard the shots, Sky was slipping through my arms and bullets were flying by my head. I don't know who it could've been. Sky told me she was only inviting me and I told her I was only going to bring a couple homies. Maybe it was that broad Darlene from the taco shop. Maybe she followed us from the set to the beach. Or maybe it could've been some of Tiny Blue Rocc's homies trying to get retaliation for killing Tiny Awol, but even if that was true, how did they know we were there? Sky promised me she wouldn't invite anyone else and the way she hopped in my arms when I arrived showed me she wouldn't set me up. Plus, why would she put her own self in danger? That doesn't make any sense to me.

Arm & Hammer broke the silence. "I think I know who it was." Pernell and I turned and looked at him.

"It was that bitch ass rip nigga who got that baby blue Caprice on them gay ass spinning rims."

"How the fuck do you know?" Pernell asked as he paced in the living room.

Arm & Hammer continued on. "I thought I b'd it at the light when faggot blood over there was all hugged up on that bitch, thinkin' there wasn't a fuckin' worry in the world."

I knew exactly whose car Arm & Hammer was describing. "That's Cowboys'," I blurted out. I remembered seeing it parked at the beach the day of the Puerto Rican Fest next to Tiny Blue Rocc and his homies; and it was out front of the liquor store the day they jumped me.

Arm & Hammer roared up again. "I told you niggas! If you would've listened to me and just bicked it, none of this would've ever happened, and Boguard would still be here!"

Pernell tried to stop Arm & Hammer before he rattled off any more blame on me. "Look P funk, it is what it is. It happened, now we gotta figure it out and get brackin'."

"Pernell, what is it? What do you have to figure out? What are you talking about?" Krystal stood in the hallway, her belly protruding from her nightgown. The wells of her eyes were starting to fill up with tears. "I thought you said-"

Pernell quickly cut her off. "Baby, go back to sleep. This ain't got nothin' to do with you."

Krystal didn't budge. The tears that were sitting hostage in her eyes were now running down her cheeks. Her left hand kept rubbing her belly like it was a magical lamp. Her disappointment was heard in the shakiness of her voice. "Pernell, please don't be doing anything stupid. You promised me that you wouldn't jeopardize our family."

Pernell took a deep breath and let it out slowly. His eyes darted at her and then at us then back to her again. He took ten steps to Krystal, kissed her cheek then down on her belly. "Look baby, I'm not finna jeopardize anything, but you know what it is. Now, how bout you go back to sleep?" Pernell rubbed her belly. "Little man doesn't need his momma stressin'."

Pernell flashed his million dollar smile hoping that would help but Krystal closed her eyes, and when she opened them, there was something missing. The affection that sat in her eyes had vanished. She was no longer looking at Pernell; she was looking through him. Pernell wrapped his arm around Krystal's waist and escorted her back to the bedroom. When he returned he had a black plastic footlocker with him that was about four and a half feet long.

I held my breath and my heart followed as I watched Pernell open the locker. The inside of the foot locker was meticulously organized from top to bottom. The two 4x4 trays unfolded as he opened the locker all the way. The tray closest to me had enough clips and ammunition to make Rambo jealous while the other tray had two semi-automatic 9mm's sitting perfectly next to each other. Pernell placed a 9mm with an extended clip on the coffee table that sat in front of the TV. "That's for you, D."

I didn't say a word. I grabbed the pistol and checked the clip to make sure it was full then I took the empty .45 that was still tucked in my waist and threw it on the couch behind us. The 9mm looked like something that belonged in the video game, Halo. I tried stuffing it in my waist but the end of the clip stuck out from underneath my shirt.

Pernell reached into the foot locker and removed the trays so he could have room to pull out the next items. In his hand were two bulletproof vests, each one had a rectangular patch across the chest that read SDPD. Arm & Hammer made a gesture with his head towards me. "Since blood got us in this funk, he don't need one." I wasn't going to argue with him over that, he was right. I should've listened earlier and maybe none of us would be in this situation right now.

Pernell kept fumbling through his box of goodies until he pulled out a black TEC-9 with a gold muzzle attached to it and slid it across the coffee table. Arm & Hammer looked at it like there was shit spread across the handle and pushed it back across the coffee table to Pernell. "I don't give a fuck how brackin' that muthafucka look, I'm bool. They stay jammin' and I ain't tryin' to get murked out there." Arm & Hammer pulled out his Desert Eagle. "I'm still finna use this bitch. I just need more bullets. You got anything for her?"

Pernell threw Arm & Hammer a box of ammo from the tray on the couch and picked up the TEC-9 and held it to the light. "Fuck it my nigga I'll use her. I'll show you how to get active with it." Pernell took his red bandana, thumbed out every bullet in the clip, wiped them down and reloaded them. When he finished, he looked at me then Arm & Hammer. "Load up, my niggas, it's time to get brackin'."

Tiny Blue Rocc

Chapter 39

—•••—

I can't believe it's come down to this, me needing to kill Deshaun. Cuz is like my cousin, his Uncle Juney is like an uncle to me. When Lil Blue Rocc would be locked up somewhere, instead of me kicking it with the homies I would go to Uncle Juney's house and post up over there with him and Deshaun. Truth be told, Juney was like the hood's uncle. He never did mind having us over at his house. He would always tell us he'd rather us be in the house than outside where the police could harass us.

Up until this summer, when I saw Deshaun at the Puerto Rican Fest with that bitch ass nigga Young Active, he and I were tighter than a seals pussy. Four summers straight, we had a routine that never switched. He would get dropped off at his Uncle Juney's house at 7:30 am by his mom before she went to work and I would be over there by 8. Uncle Juney would have already left the house to collect the debts from the numbers he was still running throughout the South East. Me and Deshaun would hop on the PlayStation for a few games of Madden 'til it hit noon and like clockwork that's when he'd help me sack up my AZ weed I got from Carlos. I remember Deshaun was so fucking square that first summer he thought weed was oregano. The nigga was an L7 but he was always a stand up dude. It didn't matter what was going on, he never switched up on me. His loyalty to our friendship was like mine to the hood; good, bad, or indifferent. It didn't matter. It was loyalty before dishonor.

It was the second summer of him getting dropped off at his uncle's house that I remember taking him to get his dick wet for the first time. I had just turned 13 and for the last month, I was smashing on this fine ass Cambodian chick whose family moved in the corner house on 49th and Hilltop, right across from the park. She was three years older and a cold freak. Her name was Porsha and she let me do whatever I wanted as long as I brought her a Phillies Titan blunt packed to the rim with the fire AZ I had on deck, and a bottle of Blue Raspberry Mad Dog 20/20. She would smoke half the blunt, drink half the bottle and then it was on from there.

I think it was the Friday before my grandparents took me to my first family reunion in Texarkana that I asked Deshaun if he had ever seen some real pussy before. His response to me was comedy, "Yea, I've seen one before, in one of my dad's magazines that he hides from me and my mom underneath his bed. It was disgusting. It sort of looked like that hairy character from the Adams Family, Cousin Itt." I couldn't stop laughing when I heard that shit.

Deshaun and I had a gang of memories like that, he was my nigga in those days but none of that mattered now. The line was crossed when he chose sides with them bitch ass niggas from across the tracks. Plus, cuz name is linked to Tiny Awol getting smoked so no matter how much love I might've had for him, that shit is long gone.

By the time we reached Big Knocc Out's house on 39th and F, Cowboy wouldn't stop cheesing. I knew exactly what he was smiling about, it was how good his aim is. "You see that shit, cuz? I got the bitch and I almost had that bitch ass nigga she was huggin' up on. If it wasn't for her faggot ass being in front of him, I would've knocced cuz off too."

I smiled because I knew he was right. Cowboy could pluck an ant off an apple from fifty yards away. His grandfather owned a shack in the Romona Mountains and we would go up there and kill coyotes with him. There would be times he would be hundred fifty yards out and still hit his target.

Cowboy parked the Caprice in the alley behind the dumpster three houses down. Once we made it to the makeshift fence that surrounded Big Knocc Out's yard, I slid a piece of sheet metal that was tucked in between the gap of the wooden fence and the stack of cinder blocks and we squeezed our way into the backyard.

Other than Blue Rocc, Big Knocc Out was my favorite OG homie. He wasn't just Cowboy's step pops, he was a gangsta. He would lace us up in all situations and whenever we needed a thang to do our thang, he never failed to point us in the right direction to cop one. Taking the blue towel off the weight bench I covered the AK the best I could that was stuffed in my pant leg when we got out the Caprice.

Cowboy walked into the house and grabbed each of us a 32 ounce of St. Ides that Big Knocc Out bought us before we left for the mission. By the time Cowboy returned I already copped a squat on the blue and white traveling cooler that sat next to the sliding glass door. Our objective was to knock off that bitch Sky first, and if we got Deshaun and his bitch ass homies then that was a bonus. I needed to get back at the bitch who tried to take my life and who got Lil Blue Rocc smoked.

I moved the cooler I was sitting on closer to his chair so he could hear me better. "You know the nigga that was hugged up on the bitch, the one you said got away?" Cowboy nodded his head yes. "That was cuz who killed Tiny Awol and I saw him run over to the gold Lexus."

Cowboy stopped grinning and took a hit of the Newport. "Is that right? I thought you hit cuz when he was running over there?"

"Nah, cuh, I missed."

Cowboy took another hit of the Newport and held the smoke in his lungs before he said another word. "You know what that means cuz?"

I took the Newport from his hand and put it to my lips and inhaled. I knew exactly what that shit meant. It meant that I was going to have to murk Deshaun, and we're going to have to put in some more work tonight. It was time to get craccin'.

Deshaun

Chapter 40

This time I'm driving the Lexus and Boguard has been replaced with Pernell. Only an hour earlier did it seem like everything was falling into place, homies were giving me my props for putting in work on Tiny Awol and the three of us were on our way to see my future baby momma. Then everything got fucked up, fast. In a blink of an eye Sky and Boguard were both dead and it's my fucking fault.

Arm & Hammer tapped my shoulder from the backseat and pointed at the exit. "Blood, get off on Market and bang that left. We might be able to catch a nigga leavin' the liquor store by the motorcycle club." While I waited for the light to turn green, the streets looked deserted. There wasn't a person in sight, let alone a dope fiend on any corner. It was only 11:30 pm and this area was usually alive on a Saturday night. In all my summers hanging out at my Uncle Juney's house, I'd never seen it this quiet.

Arm & Hammer kept directing me as the light turned green and I made a right onto 42nd. The liquor store on the right brought back memories of me having my first sip of alcohol. I was 14 and I was with

Tiny Blue Rocc and his cousins and they wanted me to distract Oscar behind the counter as they ran out of the liquor store with two 5 gallon bottles of Carlo Rossi. As crazy as I thought that was for me three years ago I was in a whole other ball game now.

Pernell sat straight up in the passenger seat and pointed at the guy leaving the liquor store holding a brown paper bag in the cuff of his forearm like a football. "We got us one."

I made sure to keep the Lexus far enough down the block so he wouldn't notice us following him. It probably wouldn't have mattered how close we got because he was too engulfed in his conversation on the phone to pay any attention to us stalking him from behind. Arm & Hammer pulled his Desert Eagle out from his waist and put it on his lap. "I bet you blood finna head to that house on Denby. We can catch blood as he makes the right on F."

The tiny knots in my stomach began to tighten as I watched the guy in the white t-shirt make the right onto F. "Kill the lights and park up there." Pernell pointed up the street to a yellow house that was directly on the corner of 42nd and F. He pulled the hood of his sweater over his head and put on his black

Nike gloves, then placed the TEC-9 across his lap and checked the clip for the last time.

Before I even came to a complete stop, Arm & Hammer was already out of the car power walking to catch up to his victim. Pernell looked at me and gave me my instructions before he hopped out and followed Arm & Hammer. "We finna be right back, so be ready. If you see any funny shit, shoot."

I leaned my chair back as far as I could so that my eyes could only see over the dash. I didn't need anyone noticing me while I sat in the car and watched their backs. By the time the guy got off his cell phone, Pernell and Arm & Hammer were no more than twenty steps behind. Arm & Hammer's voice was loud and clear enough for me to hear through the passenger window. "Aye, my nigga, what's craccin'? Doesn't Veronica stay right here?" Arm & Hammer pointed to the yellow house that was behind him.

"Who the fuck is you niggas, cuz?"

Pernell smiled. "C'mon cuz, you actin' like you don't remember me." Pernell double patted his chest. "I'm C Face's cousin. I met you at the park last year. I'm from Eight Tray Gangstas. Don't Veronica still stay right here?" Pernell nodded to the same house Arm & Hammer pointed at.

"I don't know that bitch, cuz! And, nigga, who the fuck is C Face? I don't know you cuz!"

I've never seen a smile so big come across Arm & Hammer's face. He looked at Pernell and without breaking his smile, spoke. "I told you cuz won't know shit." Like some Jedi mind trick, the two pulled out their pistols simultaneously. Arm & Hammer's trigger finger was a hair faster than Pernell's and his first bullet ripped through the white t-shirt right above the heart, and the next three shots exploded through the center of his chest. Pernell squeezed his trigger as the body in front of them went stumbling backwards into the street. The eruption from the TEC-9 woke up the block. Alarms from the cars parked in front and behind me went screaming in the night like someone came by and kicked their doors. Porch lights on the block started to turn on.

I lowered my window and only stuck out my mouth. "You niggas hurry the fuck up!"

I put the car in drive but held my foot on the break as Pernell and Arm & Hammer sprinted back to the Lexus. Arm & Hammer dove in and laid across the back seat and Pernell jumped in the front, tossed the TEC under his seat and slapped the dashboard. "Hurry up D, back to the set!"

My foot was still glued to the brake when what Pernell said to me finally registered. He must think this shit is over. So they smoke one muthafucka and I'm supposed to drive us back to the set like it's even? Fuck that. I stared directly into Pernell's eyes as I spoke. "Listen my nigga, you got me fucked up if you think I'm finna drive us back to the set after only this. They killed Boguard, took Sky from me and damn near killed me and Arm & Hammer and you think we're done, nigga?"

Arm & Hammer must've felt what I was saying because he over spoke me. "Blood is right, Y.A." Pernell swiveled his body to look at Arm & Hammer now sitting behind me. "We ain't finished yet, we need mo' than one ru."

Pernell pulled the TEC back out from under his seat and loaded another clip. "Fuck it, I guess we all in."

I let my foot off the brake, smashed on the gas, and made a left onto F Street towards 39th. I glanced at

Pernell. "You muthafuckin' right we all in, nigga; ain't no other way to be."

Chapter 41

Quail was the next street we crossed and I knew we were close. Big Knocc Out's house was only a block away. During those summers at Uncle Juney's, Tiny Blue Rocc would drag me over here with him so he could re-up on fruits, as he liked to call it, so he could hustle and smoke throughout the day. The white building that doubled as a home resembled an old warehouse. It was pure concrete and it honestly didn't fit in with the rest of the homes on the block. It sat directly on the corner of 39th and F and its best days were long fucking gone.

There was a small opening in the makeshift fence between the corrugated sheet metal and half-built wall of cinder blocks that Tiny Blue Rocc would stand at, knock three times, stick his hand through the hole and get his sack. It never mattered what time we got there, there was always someone on the other side of that fence giving him what he came for.

I parked a quarter block east of the house behind a primered Camaro. The block looked quiet, there was no movement anywhere. Sitting there in silence I knew what needed to happen. We needed our revenge, our get back for what they did to Boguard, and I needed my revenge for them taking Sky from me. Even though I was all in and ready for what was about to happen I could still feel it, that gnawing sensation in the pit of my stomach. It was there that night at the taco shop when I shot at Darlene and it was there that night I shot Tiny Awol in the face while he was in his car. That feeling never seems to go away, and now it's here again burying itself deep into my abdomen.

I pointed to the house ahead of us. "Ya'll see that arm-sized hole between those cinder blocks and sheet metal?" Pernell and Arm & Hammer both nodded. "There's usually someone posted on the other side of it every day, all day long. That's the spot everyone goes to for a sack."

Pernell looked at the house in front of us and out through the back window of the Lexus and shook his head. "D, how the fuck you know somebody here? Ain't nobody out here."

"That's why nigga!" Arm & Hammer pointed at the baby blue Caprice that was parked across the street.

Without even thinking, I was the first one out of the Lexus. I pulled the .45 from my waist and held it against my chest as I've seen in countless cop movies with my mom, but for some reason I knew I didn't look as confident as they did in the movies. This time the .45 felt heavier in my hand, maybe because my heart was heavier now.

I looked back at Pernell and Arm & Hammer, who were now both behind me. "Y'all ready?" The two nodded their hooded heads and I took the lead. I stayed hunched to the ground and beelined towards the hole in the makeshift fence and kept my head lower than the hole. Pernell and Arm & Hammer didn't cross the alley with me but I didn't care. They were both ten feet behind, across the alley at the other fence.

The Babylon sirens were getting closer and we didn't have long before the ghetto bird would be over the top of us. I took a step closer to the fence, held my breath, and put my ear to the plywood hoping I could hear a voice.

Arm & Hammer saw the barrel of an AK coming out the hole the same time I did. I pointed my .45 at the fence and fired and so did Arm & Hammer. The echoing ring from the Desert Eagle bounced off the alley walls. Through the spaces of the fence you could see Cowboy's face balled up each time a bullet penetrated his body. I fired three more shots, and then there was silence.

Arm & Hammer rushed over to me and gave me his hand. "You good?" I shook my head yes while I pushed myself to my feet. "Good. We gots to go. Now!" Arm & Hammer turned from me to run back to the car then all of a sudden he was lifted off his feet, like an invisible giant snatched him by his collar and threw him backwards.

Tiny Blue Rocc stood in the middle of the alley holding the long barrel .44 Magnum he bought from my Uncle Juney two summers ago. That was one of my favorite guns that my uncle used to own. Then Tiny Blue Rocc took aim at Pernell.

I fumbled the pistol in my hand before I fired my first shot at the Milwaukee Brewer logo that sat in the center of Tiny Blue Rocc's hat. But still faster than he could pull his trigger on Pernell. My shot was wide and hit the dumpster to his left. Tiny Blue Rocc then turned the extra-long barrel at me. I didn't stop squeezing my finger until the clip was empty. The last two bullets that left my barrel hit Tiny Blue Rocc in the center of his chest above his stomach. His legs buckled and his body folded in half as he fell to the concrete.

To the right of me, Arm & Hammer was still on the ground. His eyes were closed but his hands were moving frantically across his chest. Three holes were perfectly placed in the center of his hoodie and I could hardly hear him as his lips continued to move.

Out of instinct, I reached for the chest of his hoodie and tried lifting him to his feet when something solid pressed against my hands. It was the vest he put on earlier. The relief in his eyes when I was able to get him to his feet and back to the Lexus was priceless. I jumped through the passenger window and laid the seat flat, while Arm & Hammer laid flat in the back. We needed it to look like Pernell was by himself, not with a group of hooded individuals. Pernell smashed on the pedal so hard it spun the tires before we peeled off. His voice was hard to hear over the Piru Love blasting in the speakers. "Y'all niggas good?!"

I nodded my head and Arm & Hammer's voice came loud and clear from the back seat. "Yea, I'm bool. Luckily I have this vest on."

Detective Braveheart

Chapter 42

The shit I was looking at wasn't supposed to carry itself out here to the beach. These monkeys knew that this area was off-limits. They can shoot and kill each other in their fucking hoods but they weren't supposed to bring that niggerish bullshit out here to the beach where all the God-loving Americans go.

The blue plastic cups laying in the sand must have been dropped when the gunfire started, and probably belonged to the three half naked girls huddled together in an oversized blue blanket. I don't understand these nigger bitches. They come outside half-dressed, get drunk and high, hangout with any ol' Tom, Dick and Harry then someone comes and shoots at them for whatever dumb ass reason, someones dies, and now they're surprised. Their stupidity fucking kills me.

"Detective, over here." One of the uniform officers was standing over a body lying in a bonfire pit. There was something about the smell of burning flesh that I could never get used to, it's a smell you can't erase from your memory by any stretch of the imagination.

I remember the first time I came across that smell. It was my second week in GSU and we had a Mexican gang member from Logan Heights named Tripper surrounded at his girlfriend's house in Lomita Village. He was wanted for killing two junior high students a week earlier for no fucking reason at all. We found his piece of shit ass holed up in his girlfriend's house with her and her six-year-old daughter. Witnesses said he was in there already for about ten hours. When we arrived, for the safety of the mother and child, we kept our distance. But by the fourth hour of us being there, the Captain had enough and gave us the OK to kick in the door. Before we could cross the street, the whole house went up in flames. It was like the son of a bitch had the house drenched in gasoline. All we could do was wait for the fire department and watch the house melt in front of us. I could hear the cries from the mother and daughter through the crackling of the fire as it ripped through the house. The earthy smell mixed with bubbling fat from their burning flesh snaked its way across the street and into my nose. The smell of human flesh wasn't as sweet as deer meat, this stench made me want to spew my lunch all over the sidewalk.

The smell entering my nostrils now was no different from fifteen years ago. It didn't matter if it was beaner meat or nigger meat, it all smelt the same. My partner kept the uni's out of my way as I examined the body. It looks like his dumb ass didn't see the shots coming. The entry wound that entered above his left ear was the size of a lemon and it exited through his right eye. His back must have been towards the bridge when they started shooting.

After a five minute conversation with the rookie beat cop, my partner made his way next to me at the bonfire pit. "Isn't that Melvin Baker?"

I knew the face looked familiar. We pulled this fucker and a couple of his friends over on Skyline Drive a couple of months back for no license plate. If I'm not mistaken, he was known as Boguard in the streets. Why in the fuck did they call him that? I have no fucking clue. But the real question is, why was he out here with our other dead victim Monica "Sky" Brooks. She parades around town with a lot of gang members, so why did he trust her?

Before I found the answer to my question, the walkie-talkies on the uniform cops all exploded with the same news. Two dead and one in critical condition in the Mount Hope area. I looked over at Whitehead who was taking a picture of a woman's sprawled out body in the sand and waved to get his attention. "I bet that these two fuckers and the three over on Market will help us put the pieces of this puzzle together."

By the time we reached 39th Street, there was a congregation of bystanders around the yellow tape on the corner of the alley. The many different faces I saw surrounding the body meant whoever was under that sheet was some sort of big shot around here.

An officer walked up breathing heavily as though he walked a mile to get here. "Looking good, old friend. Talk to me. What do we have here?" I haven't seen Ricketts in over fifteen years. He was my first partner when I was a beat cop but now he looks like the fat, stereotypical donut eating cop who gained the weight of a small child on his stomach.

The mucus in his lungs from all the fucking high cholesterol foods made it hard for me to decipher his words. It sounded like he was trying to suck in air as he was talking. "Braveheart, good to see you too. I still remember how you operate. No speculation, only the facts so I'll get right to the point. What has happened here is the continuation from the DOA we have down on 42nd and F. Black male, ambushed leaving the liquor store, shot multiple times in the chest and died in the middle of the street. We have a few witnesses from both crime scenes describing the same Lexus leaving."

"What color was the Lexus?" I knew what he was going to say but I needed my hunch to be confirmed.

"Some are saying brown, some are saying gold, but they all are saying it was on 20inch chrome rims."

I didn't need any more information. I knew exactly who the car belonged to. I've pulled it over three times in two weeks as it cruised down Parkside Avenue in Paradise Hills. It belongs to our C.I.'s friend, the one he brought to the park restroom a month ago. Since that meeting, I've pulled it over four more times just so I could get the information on the dick heads who were in it.

Detective Whitehead finally joined me and nudged the body under the sheet with his foot. "So, what happened here?"

Ricketts continued reading from his notepad. "According to a witness, she said the Lexus came flying up F street and parked right there." Ricketts pointed to the space behind a parked Camaro. "Three black males with hoodies and red rags on their faces got out and surrounded the house on the corner. One by the fence and the other two-"

Whitehead interrupted Ricketts in mid-sentence like he does everyone else when they try to give their version of what happened at a crime scene. My partner had some fucking weird special gift to where all he had to do was look at a scene, close his eyes then within minutes his ass would have what happened down to a science. Honestly, that was why I recruited him to be my partner. I'll take any extra advantage I can to get these monkeys off the streets.

Ricketts was ready to open his mouth again but it wasn't necessary, Whitehead already ran the scenario down to me. We walked a few feet to the alley where the paramedics were loading a man on a gurney through the double doors of their ambulance. "You think he's going to make it?"

"It doesn't look good, Detective. He's already lost a ton of blood."

Whitehead gave me that look and I knew what was running through his mind. It was time for us to go. "Are you thinking what I'm thinking?"

Before he could ask me another question, I was pressing talk on our C.I.'s phone number. "Where are you? We need to talk. Now."

Deshaun

Chapter 43

Walking up the stairs to Krystal's apartment seemed like they would never end. I couldn't erase the images of Tiny Blue Rocc's body dropping in the alley where we used to hang out and smoke weed. Seconds before I pulled the trigger the bewilderment in his eyes almost made me hesitate but I had no other choice. It was either shoot him or let Pernell die. I did what I had to do.

Arm & Hammer's giddiness brought me back to reality. He shot the P into my right hand, as we reached the top of the stairs. "That's the shit I'm talkin' about, nigga. That's how you perform out there!"

Pernell turned toward us and put his finger over his lips for us to be quiet as he opened the front door. To our surprise, Krystal was sitting on the couch watching the news. The ducts of her eyes were filled with tears. "You promised me you wouldn't do anything like this again." Krystal burst into tears and threw the lighter that was on the coffee table at Pernell's chest.

Pernell stood in the living room stone-faced. If it wasn't for the fact that I was just with him then I would've believed him. Pernell picked the lighter off the brown shag carpet and acted as if nothing happened and sat next to Krystal on the couch. "Promise you what, Krystal? What the fuck are you talking about now?"

Krystal didn't say another word. She picked up the remote control and turned the volume up. It was Kimberly Hunt from Channel 10 News.

There were two shooting incidents only hours apart that took the lives of four teens and left one in critical condition. During the early evening of this beautiful Labor Day weekend, a young man and woman were shot to death while enjoying a bonfire at the bay by the Dana Hotel in Mission Beach. Authorities are saying that the two shooters parked across the street and opened fire on the group, killing two.

An hour later, and 10 miles to the east in the Mount Hope community, violence struck again. Gunfire mortally wounded two males and landed another in critical condition. SDPD says it looks to be gang-related. They are expressing to the public, if anyone has any information regarding the shootings, please contact the Crime Stoppers hotline.

Krystal turned the TV off and threw the remote at Pernell. "That's what I'm talking about, Pernell!" Krystal stood up and her tears fell onto her pregnant belly. Pernell didn't say a word. He sat there looking at Krystal, emotionless to her sobs. "You promised me you wouldn't jeopardize our family."

Pernell stood up and placed his hands on the side of Krystal's shoulders as he stood. "Look Krystal, I don't know what the fuck you're talkin' about. Just cause you saw somethin' on the news doesn't mean it was me or the homies. You're trippin' right now."

Krystal slapped Pernell's hands off her shoulders and turned her back to him. "Don't ever touch me again, Pernell! I ain't stupid." Krystal walked to the patio door and stood there silent. Her curly black hair looked like waves moving along her back as she tried to stop crying. Her soft defeated voice echoed off the glass door in front of her. "How could you jeopardize our soon to be family like this Pernell? You probably won't even be here to watch our son be born."

Pernell stretched out his arm for Krystal to come back to him but she still wasn't looking at him. "Krystal, why in the fuck is you trippin'? Everything is all good. I ain't goin' nowhere. I promise."

"Yeah right. You are going to be going somewhere. You're gonna leave us and get locked up because you love your friends and your set more than you do us."

Pernell's poker face finally cracked. The gangsta that just shot and killed a man thirty minutes ago was no longer standing in front of me. Pernell's voice lost some of its bravado as he walked towards the patio to Krystal. "Look, I promise you I'm good, Krys. Ain't nothin' finna happen to me, on everything. Now go back to bed and I'll be there in a minute."

Watching Pernell walk Krystal into the bedroom, Kimberly Hunt's voice was on autopilot in my ears. *"Gunfire mortally wounded two males and landed another in critical condition. SDPD says it looks to be gang-related. They are expressing to the public, if anyone has any information regarding the shootings, please contact the Crime Stoppers hotline."*

Her words didn't affect Arm & Hammer. He sat down on the couch in the same spot as he was before we left, pulled his Desert Eagle from his jeans, popped the clip, racked the slide, and started to dismantle it so he could clean it.

My thoughts however were all over the place. I could hardly think, let alone sit down. My adrenaline was drying up and reality was setting in. Two men mortally wounded and one in critical condition sounds like twenty-five years to life if we're caught. I took a swig of Hennessy we left on the kitchen counter to wet my mouth. "Arm & Hammer, are we good? You think anyone saw us?"

Arm & Hammer laughed at my question. "Hell muthafuckin' yea we straight! That news shit ain't nothin' new to us, huh Y.A.?"

Behind me, Pernell was exiting the bedroom but he didn't answer. He hadn't said a word since his last lie to Krystal by the patio door. He took the Hennessey and chugged it like it was water. His eyes lost a bit of their valor since returning from the bedroom. "D, good lookin' back there. I didn't even…" Pernell's voice trailed off as he took another shot and walked to the sliding glass door. "On the set, you saved a nigga out there. I owe you one."

"Y.A., don't even trip. It is what it is. I just did what y'all niggas taught me to do. Remember, I'm the one who got us in this bullshit." I walked over to the dining table, took the blunt we left in the ashtray, sparked it, and blew a cloud the size of Texas over the living room. "I can't believe that Boguard is gone. We gotta call his mom and let the big homies know what just happened."

Pernell snatched the blunt from my hand. "We ain't finna say a muthafuckin' word about tonight to anyone. Not even to the big homies."

What the fuck was Pernell talking about? Rule number seven was to always inform the big homies when something popped off so they could filter that information to the rest of the set. According to P-Nutt, we never want any homies in the set blind to what's happening.

"Y.A.'s right, D." Arm & Hammer stood up from the couch. He was done cleaning his Desert Eagle and already slid it back into his waist. "Muthafuckas already know who be puttin' in all the work around here. We ain't gotta tell nobody shit. What's understood ain't got to be said."

Chapter 44

The walk from Krystal's apartments back to my apartments normally took eight minutes but this time it doubled because I didn't want to be seen by anyone, let alone the babylons. I made sure to walk through all the nooks and crannies that Pernell showed me and I avoided walking under any street lights.

Outside my front door, I pressed my ear on the cold wood trying to gauge how asleep my mom was on the couch. Since we moved here she hasn't slept in the bedroom one time. Her gasp for air while she slept meant I had to be extra quiet. For some odd reason even though my mom snored like a hibernating bear, she had some sort of special power that only a mother could have. It didn't matter how loud her snoring was, she could hear a mouse piss on cotton and that would wake her up.

Taking my Id from my wallet I slid it into the gap of the door and the jam until it touched the barrel of the lock. After a couple jiggles on the doorknob and a little bit of pressure, the handle turned all the way and I was inside. I picked up that trick hanging out with

Slim a few times while I was on the lookout for when he broke into houses.

Our living room, which was usually jet black in the wee hours of the morning, was illuminated by an infomercial that was replaying on the TV. My mom laid on the couch covered in a small blanket I gave her on Mother's Day two years ago that had some of my pictures woven into the squares. She must've fallen asleep waiting for me to come home. I knew I was going to get my ass chewed out tomorrow, but that is nothing compared to the consequences I'll face if I were arrested for what happened tonight.

With each miniature step across the living room, I held my breath. The floors here bowed when you walked and always let out a tiny squeak underneath your feet to let everyone in the house know there was movement. The light from the TV was like my flashlight that guided me through the hallway. All I wanted was to get in my room, take my clothes off and go to sleep. And hope the shit I just witnessed and committed didn't follow me in my dreams.

A voice I wasn't too familiar with hearing anymore echoed off the walls behind me. The strength in his voice was something I used to cherish but now the lack of it fell on deaf ears. I haven't seen him since we moved here and now he wants to act like he has something to say to me. He wasn't even supposed to be here right now. "I know you hear me Deshaun. Where the hell have you been, young man?"

I turned around to see my dad standing in the middle of the hallway still draped in his khaki-colored janitorial uniform. The look on his face was one I've never seen before. The longer we stood there, the louder the slaps from the belt in his hand became. "Boy, you hear me?! Where the fuck have you been?"

I still didn't say a word, for what, what was I supposed to say? I just stood there waiting for his next question. I leaned my shoulder against the wall with my arms crossed. With what I just went through, there was nothing he could tell me or anything I wanted to hear from him. If he would have never lost his job I wouldn't be here in this bullshit now.

From behind him my mom's voice sprinkled the situation with concern. "Son, you heard your father. Please just answer him. We just wanna make sure you're okay." My mom flipped the switch in the hallway and it took a couple of seconds for my eyes to adjust to the light. I've been operating in darkness for the last handful of hours. The light seemed foreign to me.

At first glance, I would've sworn my mom's face was stuck like that. Her mouth stretched vertically up to her eyes, her hands clutched the collar of her robe as she pulled it tighter like there was a breeze in the hallway. At times my mom was overdramatic but when I looked at my pop's face I knew it was something serious. I've never seen him shaken up. He only had two moods: anger or nonchalant, but never disbelief. "Son, what the fuck is that?"

I followed the direction of his finger and glanced down at my clothes. From the chest of my hoodie down along my jeans was completely stained with blood, Sky's blood. I totally forgot that I held Sky in my arms as she died in the sand.

Standing there I felt like a complete stranger in front of my parents. No longer was I the fresh-faced straight-A kid who had aspirations to go college and follow in my dad's footsteps. I was now a gang member, someone who now had no regard for human life let alone his own. There was no need to answer any of my dad's questions; they knew what was all over my clothes. It was time for them to come to grips with who they turned me into.

Walking into my room, my pictures of my old life where I lived worry free in Point Loma were all around me, reminding me of how simple life was before we moved. My mom even hung the first place award Lee and I won at the Engineering World Competition from the year before, but none of that meant anything now. All that mattered was getting out of these stained clothes and finding a way to get rid of them.

Before I was able to get all my clothes off, my bedroom door swung open and my pops stood in the center of my doorway. His confidence was back in place and this time he didn't ask me shit, he just told me what I needed to do. "Hurry up, get undressed and hand me those clothes. We gotta get this shit out of the house - fast." My dad picked up the hoodie I threw over my chair in the corner of the room and started stuffing everything into a black trash bag.

He tied up the bag and threw it in the hallway. "Deshaun, you don't have to answer me but I want you to know what I know. Your uncle called us and said the word in his neighborhood was you were around there when the shootings took place by his house. He also said he didn't know if the police knew yet, but the witnesses in the neighborhood were describing you and your friends leaving the scene in a Lexus."

I opened my mouth to tell him about Sky and the bonfire but he shut me up and continued on. "Son, I love you but whatever you've done, I'm not condoning it. At all! But I'm still not finna hand you over to no white folks either. We will figure this shit out together, but for now..." I looked at my pops through the hole of my new shirt I was pulling over my head. "You're going to stay with my sister, Jaleen, in Oakland. Your mom is gonna take you to the Greyhound while I get rid of this shit."

The thought of my dad and mom helping me leave town and getting rid of my clothes concerned me. If the police found out they could be charged with aiding and abetting. I don't know how much time that carries but I don't want them to be caught up in any of my bullshit. "Dad, you don't have---"

"Listen up son, I know what I don't have to do but you're my son regardless of what you've done." My pops gave me a reassuring look and rushed me to the front door where my mom was waiting with her keys dangling from one hand and a bible in another. His voice reached my ears for the last time that night. "Deshaun, I love you. Be safe up there and just so you know, this ain't my first rodeo."

Chapter 45

My moms and pops were so caught up in getting me out of San Diego, they didn't give me any information on what to do once I got to Oakland. Mind you, I've never met my dad's sister, he rarely spoke of her. I've only seen a picture of her once. The picture was in a shoebox stacked against the corner of the garage labeled 'junk' before we moved. It was of my dad, her and Uncle Juney, they must have all been in their early teens because they were standing in front of the YMCA. My dad had his arm wrapped over his sister's shoulder who stood in the middle of my dad and Uncle Juney. It had to be around the summertime because my dad and uncle didn't have a shirt on, their sister had on a one-piece bathing suit with a pair of shorts to cover the bottom half of her body. She looked identical to my dad, from her posture even to her face structure. Both of their mouths had a unique curl that went upwards to their eyebrows when they smiled. I remember asking my dad if they were twins and he only smiled at my question. To this day I never understood why I never met her.

"Deshaun," I heard my name float across the linoleum floors. A woman with a black tank top and an African-colored dashiki skirt stood under the exit sign. A Virginia Slim hung from her pressed lips while she motioned with her finger for me to come towards her. Everything about her resembled my pops, from her athletic frame to her well-manicured afro. They were spitting images of each other.

I walked where her finger was directing me and put my duffle bag on the row of chairs that were behind her. "What's up young blood?" She made a fist so I could give her a pound. "Glad to see you made it. You might wanna pick up your bag before one of these jay cats takes off running with it."

My Auntie Jaleen turned around, walked out of the bus station and didn't say another word to me. I stood there for a second admiring her good looks. She had to be every bit of sixty years old and she still had it going on. *I guess black doesn't crack*, I thought to myself as I followed her out of the station to the platinum colored Jaguar she parked across the street.

"When you get in, lean the seat all the way back." I nodded my head in agreement. I knew the drill. "You never know who's watching."

I don't know if the air conditioning didn't work or if she just didn't feel it was hot enough, but my shirt kept sticking to my back as if I lathered up with a handful of glue instead of lotion. The inside of her car smells exactly like Slims garage, skunky. The fresh scent from the weed mixed well with my auntie's Chanel N°5, reminded me of Sky.

Sky never stepped outside without dousing herself in some kind of perfume or body spray. She was like a walking incense. Everywhere she went you knew she was there by the fragrance she left. Fucked up part about it all was that last night was the last time I'll ever smell her again. I shut my eyes tight to stop them from watering.

"Is you listenin', little nigga?!" My auntie's weathered hand slapped the top of the dashboard. "Pay attention! I ain't talkin' for my health." She tipped the Virginia Slim in her left hand out her window. "Remember, you ain't my nephew and my name isn't Jaleen, it's Shavon. And you…" She pushed my temple with her pointer finger. "…are a foster kid who needs a place to stay while you transition in between homes."

The house she stopped in front of was a beaten-down craftsman that sat on 51st and 8th, next to an auto body shop that doubled as someone's home. The layers of green and vanilla paint were slowly releasing their grip from the exterior of the house. The front door looked like it had a block of cement plaster in its place.

I didn't know what to expect before I walked in but the inside of the house was completely different from the outside. I guess the saying is true, never judge a book by its cover. The jasmine fragrance from the incense burning in the kitchen tickled my nostrils as it made its way through the bamboo beads that hung in the doorway. Paintings of great African American leaders, dead and alive, lined the walls. She even had The Last Supper picture with Jesus hung over the mantle of her brick fireplace, but unlike I've seen before, every disciple and Jesus were black. In so many ways her house reminded me of my uncle's. The sense of knowing one's self and black pride was prevalent in both homes. I guess that's how it was back then and they never deviated from it. That's probably why my generation is so fucked up now. We have no sense of self.

The pumpkin-colored velvet couch in between the two oversized lamps in the middle of the living room looked like a great place to sit. The house was well kept but there was nothing new. Everything looked like it was still in the '70s. In front of me on the coffee table was a fanned out stack of Time magazines with famous black people on the covers. I picked the first one on the edge and started reading. The cover had the great political leader Tom Mboya from Kenya on it but before getting to the meat and potatoes of the article, my auntie came strutting from the kitchen with a small manila envelope the size of the Bible in her hand. "When your mom called and told me you were coming, I got these made for you."

I pinched the butterfly tabs on the back of the envelope together, unfolded the tab, and removed the items that were inside. In my hands was a new identity. I had a new name, Corey Lumpkin. I was now nineteen with a new birth certificate, a new social security card and a California driver's license. I don't know how she did it in a matter of 12 hours but she did, and the boa constrictor that was wrapped around my chest finally started to loosen its grip. I felt my chest exhale the pressure as I was finally able to breathe again.

Auntie Jaleen stuck the end of her extra long Virginia Slim on top of the mantle. "Fix your face, nephew. This is the least I can do for you. I owe my brother my life. If it wasn't for him taking that case for me and moving me up here to Oakland when we were teens, I would be in someone's prison right now for who knows how long."

The story that followed out of my auntie's lips was a trip. I never knew my pops was on trial for a murder he didn't commit. All he ever talked about was playing football in college and being an engineer. Maybe that's why he was fired. Maybe it finally came to light. Auntie Jaleen carried on with her story. "The only reason your father was released was because the murder victims girlfriend testified on his behalf. She told the jury that your dad was an innocent bystander and the shots came from a woman in the alley."

My mouth dropped. "Why didn't my dad tell me any of this? Why not tell me he was wrongfully charged and arrested?" I don't get why he kept this part of his life a secret but before I could ask any more questions, Auntie Jaleen got up from the couch and threw her cigarette into the fireplace and dabbed out the incense. "Get you some rest nephew...I know you gotta be tired after the long ass trip. We will chop it up some more tomorrow morning. Goodnight."

I kicked my shoes off and leaned my head on the arm rest of the couch. I closed my eyes and wished when I woke up that all this shit was just a bad dream.

Detective Braveheart

Chapter 46

—◆◆◆—

"Where the fuck have you two been?!"

Standing in the middle of Cap's office getting berated about how I do my fucking job was getting as old as the Motorola pager he still wears on his busted hip. I've been doing this for almost twenty years now and he continues to talk to me like I'm a fucking newbie. He's retiring in 113 days and I wished it were yesterday, I can't wait to see his ass walk out the door and not come back. As soon as he's gone I'll be on the other side of that desk barking out orders and questioning evidence in front of me. Whitehead looked to me to speak. He always wanted me to break the hard news to Cap before he spoke so he could be the good cop. "Sorry Cap, we were with our C.I."

Knowing Cap for the last fifteen years I knew my answer was about to ruffle his feathers. Standard protocol is to never leave an active crime scene until it's secured, but fuck that. If I followed every protocol and every fucking procedure in the book I wouldn't have the most arrests for the last 10 years running. And no one ever minds when the news is glorifying the department for what a great job I've been doing cleaning up the streets. The sour looking expression on Cap's face was raising my blood pressure by the millisecond.

Whitehead stepped in front of me to stop me from blowing my fucking wig, and handed Cap a 14k gold Figaro necklace with a diamond-encrusted cross hanging from it. In the center of the cross was a half carat single diamond that was embedded on top of a microscopic microphone recorder that my navy seal buddy Brian Betencourt gave me last year.

Cap held the necklace out in front of him with a ballpoint pen. "What the fuck is this shit? Detective, I'm not a fucking pawnshop and neither are you two dipshits!"

It took every ounce of respect I had left for the captain for me not to spit out what I really wanted to say. He was too out of date to understand what he had in front of him. These types of tactics are why I'm the best at what I do. I don't give a fuck how the job gets done as long as it gets done. "Sir, what you're holding out in front of you is our gift to you. That right there is the confession from our shooters today." Cap held the necklace higher above his head. "Sir, the necklace is a mobile voice recorder. The device is in the middle of the cross underneath the diamond. The microphone can record up to fifty feet in diameter."

"Get to the point, Detective."

Whitehead cut me off. "Well Captain, while we were playing fuck around with our C.I., we listened to the recordings and it sounds like we have the suspects talking about what took place at the bonfire and then the retaliation on 39th street."

Cap didn't say a word. His sunken blue eyes kept staring at the cross in front of him. He delicately laid the cross along his keyboard and sat back down. "This is good, you two, but it won't be able to hold up in a trial."

My partner blew up before I could and spiked his walkie-talkie onto the checkered tile floors in the captain's office. "What the fuck do you mean it won't hold up?! This is a fucking confession, Cap!"

The blotches on Cap's skin brightened to match the red in his eyes. "You better stand the fuck down, Detective, and watch your tone before you end up on desk duty for the next year!" He turned and looked at me. "We need something more than a voice recording on a cross. Braveheart, you've been doing this too damn long to know that anything on a non-state approved item will not hold up in court."

I reached into the black duffle bag that I brought in Cap's office and pulled out two evidence bags with a gun in each of them. One held a chrome .45 with a pearl handle and the other held a black Glock 9. "Is this what you mean, Captain?"

"You are goddamn right that's what I mean, Detective. Why in the fuck didn't you show me that first?"

"I wanted to build suspense."

Cap began to examine everything on his desk. There is no way on God's green earth with the evidence we presented to him that we couldn't get a warrant now and start kicking down some doors. I've gotten warrants with much less.

Cap walked to the hand carved liquor cabinet that doubled as a desk for his vintage vinyl record player, pulled out a crystal decanter three-quarters full of whiskey, and poured himself a glass. "Have you two talked to Judge Szumowski about a warrant for the suspects?"

"Come on Cap, you know we do everything by the book. We wanted to run this by you first before we went to the judge."

Cap stared into his glass and swirled the whiskey around to make a liquid tornado. "Great decision Braveheart. Run the ballistics first and get the confession off of this whatever you call it, so we can present it to the judge in one nice package." Cap handed me the two evidence bags and Whitehead picked up the gold chain. "Good job, you two. We are going to name this, Operation Giving Thanks."

Deshaun

Chapter 47

—◆◆◆—

Day 107:

I'm glad I brought you with me. Writing in you is the only thing keeping my mind from running all over the place. When I'm not getting historical lessons on black culture or a lecture on how to operate in secrecy, this is the only thing that brings a bit of normalcy to my days. Never once have you denied my entries, and my secrets on your pages never come with judgments or guilt, only openness to tell you more. But right there is the catch. When do I stop telling you everything? When will the day come that you are not in my presence and you betray me? The day you let someone else's hands open you and read what you've promised to keep for my eyes only? Maybe that day will never come, who knows? But while I do have your sole attention, I will use you as my confidant, my friend, and my place to release the demons that now haunt me. Thank you, journal.

Chapter 48

Ten days passed and I still hadn't called home. It's not like I had much time to do so anyways. Auntie Jaleen kept me busy with all the reading material she pushed on me every morning. It was never too much to read, only a couple of chapters in the morning and we would finish the day off reading four more before we called it a night. Truth be told, I loved reading. Before we moved across town, Me, Alex, and Lee had our own book club. We mostly stuck to dystopian fiction but black history always intrigued me.

This morning was the same as the last nine days. Me sitting at the dinette table in the kitchen. Auntie Jaleen behind me frying some turkey bacon and egg whites, and me reading a couple chapters from a book she selected that I read. Out the bay window in front of me was a man wrapped in a blue tarp, flapping one arm like a bird and carefully stacking Yellow Pages into a shopping cart with the other. "Auntie, is this what I should expect? Seclusion from the world?"

She walked past me and gazed out the window, searching for an answer. Her voice was soft. "Honestly Deshaun, that's a question I can't answer. I'm free, but that comes with a price I'm willing to pay. Sometimes being a prisoner of my past eats me up and I wish I were back in San Diego with you and family but that wasn't in my cards."

I sipped the orange juice she placed in front of me and took a bite of the turkey bacon. "What do you think I should do?"

Her eyebrows made a sharp 'V' above the bridge of her nose like my dad's. "The real question to ask nephew, is are you willing to pay the price?"

She's right. Am I willing to stay up here? Away from my parents, friends, and the only place I know, to become someone else and live a lie? Or do I go home? And face whatever music is playing for me, if any at all. Me being here could be an exaggeration but the only way for me to know was to hit up the homies.

***

I don't know if I wasn't brave enough or if I wasn't willing to pay the price but it took me three more days to build up enough courage to sneak out of my auntie's house, find a payphone and call home. The only working phone in a three block radius stood on a piss ridden corner east of a porn shop and directly across the street from a Vietnamese restaurant. The fog moving its way through the streets of Little Saigon was sort of a ghost-gray. It had a dingy filmy feel to it the more it blanketed me.

I pushed the quarter into the narrow slot, dialed the ten digits, and waited. No answer. My finger fished out the quarter from the trapdoor underneath the receiver and tried again. Still nothing. My foot started tapping the sidewalk and it wouldn't stop. There was only one other phone number I had memorized. "What up Slim? Where is everybody?"

"D-Hogg, what the fuck you mean where is everybody? Where the fuck have you been hidin' at, nigga, under a rock?"

Auntie Jaleen drilled in my head over the past thirteen days to never tell everyone everything, saying too much over the phone in her book was a no no. "I haven't been hidin'. I just went to visit some family for the end of summer. I tried callin' Pernell at his house then Krystal's but both times the phone just kept ringin'. Is everybody good?"

I never heard Slim's voice so high pitched before in the 4 months I've known him. "Hell nah everythang ain't good, nigga. The homie is in the bounty jail!"

My heart punched a hole through my chest and landed on the dewy sidewalk. The receiver against my ear tried following but was stopped abruptly by the metal bungee cord attached to it. I doubled over behind the phone booth hoping none of the vagabonds across the street saw what I just did. I could barely keep my legs from buckling underneath me but I knew I needed to hear more.

Slim explained to me that three days after I left town, Arm & Hammer and Pernell were arrested at Krystal's babyshower. Their charges were two counts of murder, one attempted murder, and the possession of two firearms. He said Krystal's whole apartment complex was surrounded by police. They even positioned the SWAT team across the street in the Jack In The Box parking lot. I needed to know how they found out it was them.

I could hear Slim sucking the smoke out of a blunt before he spoke. "I don't know but Arm & Hammer said someone is tellin'. He said the DA has three voices on tape talking about what happened that night."

My mind started racing about the conversations we had at Krystal's apartment. "Have you talked to Pernell yet? What did he say?"

Slim's words were muffled by his coughing. "Hell nah. That's the thing my nigga. Arm & Hammer said blood bailed out."

"How?"

"That's what Arm & Hammer was sayin'. He said their bail was set at a mill ticket and we know the homie ain't got no money like that."

Slim was right. Pernell stayed in the same apartments as me. So how in the hell did he bail out on a million dollars? None of this was making any fucking sense. "Slim, so what the fuck did Arm & Hammer say about me?"

"He said if he hadn't read the transcripts his lawyer brought him and if Pernell hadn't bailed out then you would be the one we're lookin' for."

Pernell always told me, for me to understand the streets I never have to think too deeply, everything is in plain view. If it walks like a duck, quacks like a duck then it's a duck and that duck needs to get plucked. I never thought in a million years he was going to be the duck. He taught me these rules, embedded them in me, and now he's broken the rule that trumps all rules. Thou shalt not snitch.

Chapter 49

━━◆◆◆━━

The plan was for Slim to pick me up at the Greyhound Station on 12th and Imperial in fourteen hours. During that time Slim was to gather as much information as he could to find out where Pernell might be hiding. There weren't many places he could go that we didn't already know but that was Slim's job to worry about, not mine. I had to come to grips that I have to be the one to kill my best friend. When Pernell vouched for me the day I got jumped in, it meant that I was also secretly vouching for him. What that means is, if either one of us broke any of the rules it was the other's responsibility to handle what needed to be handled.

The thing is, I never thought Pernell would break any rules. Shit, he was the one who taught me all of them. Pernell was my best friend even more so than Alex and Lee. What Pernell taught me was intangible. It was needed in this concrete jungle where one wrong move can cost you your life. He taught me how to be the predator and not the prey.

Slim was parked waiting for me by the homeless shelter across the street. He doesn't own a car so the gray Honda he was sitting in with the headlights off must've been another hot model he recently jacked. When I hopped in I made sure to have my gloves already on. I didn't need to leave any fingerprints in the car. "Slim, what's the word?"

Slim didn't say shit. He shot me the P, gave me a quick glance over then reached under the steering column and pulled out a chrome .38 double-action revolver and tossed it on my lap. The rubber handle wasn't as cold as the cylinder but it still made the hairs on my leg rise when I snuggled it in between my hip and my belt.

Slim grabbed the blunt out of the ashtray, stuck it in his mouth, hit the lights and hopped on the freeway. Slim never claimed to be the toughest homie but what he did take pride in was his driving abilities. We always joked if he wasn't black he could've had a career in NASCAR. The giant freeway sign approaching reads Briarwood Rd 2 ¾ miles. I turned the volume down on Jammin' Z90's top forty music and looked at Slim. "Where the fuck are we headed?"

"We are on our way to Krystal's parents' house. I heard Pernell has been hidin' out there."

Pernell never told me Krystal's parents lived so close and now I know why. He needed a place where he could hide that none of us knew about but how did Slim find out? Slim turned on a two-lane road that snaked up a hill with oversized homes that were made for giants. It was difficult to see further than a hundred yards because of the clouds that covered the full moon. Slim took another hit of the blunt and pointed ahead of us. "There, that's where Krystal's folks stay."

The house he pointed to was half the length of a football field and was secured by a black iron gate plated with gold trimmings. The front of the house was hidden behind four white sandstone columns that stretched over forty feet high, and the horseshoe driveway wrapped around a travertine fountain with lion heads positioned all around spitting out water.

Krystal's gold Lexus was parked behind a black Mercedes G Wagon at the end of the horseshoe. The only way onto the property was to press the intercom that was inserted into the brick column next to the front gate and I sure as hell wasn't doing that. I pinched the doobie between my thumb and forefinger and inhaled until the cherry lit up. "You sure Pernell is there?"

Slim pulled a yellow and black Nextel phone out of his Levi's pocket and held a small rectangle button on the side of the phone. It was the new chirp phone I saw on a commercial a couple of months back. The phone made a chirping sound like a walkie talkie before Slim spoke. "Is he in there?"

After another chirp, a males voice I didn't recognize answered. "Roger that."

Detective Braveheart

Chapter 50

—••◆••—

One thing about my partner is he needs to know every fucking bit of information before he can see the end picture. If there was a play-by-play instruction manual on every situation in the field, he would have it, read it, and live by it. I knew he was a by-the-book guy but I wish he'd just shut the fuck up for once with all the damn hypothetical questions. I knew what I wanted when I hand-picked him myself, but he was still green and if he wanted the real convictions that move you up the ladder it wasn't going to be by the damn book. All that by the book shit the captain was talking about the other day was only a formality to me. I only agreed to that bullshit so I could keep Cap out of my business and keep Internal Affairs off my ass. The shit we do out here in the field can't be played by some imaginary rule book that some suit and tie motherfucker wrote while sitting behind his desk. To play the game out here there are no rules, and that's the only rule.

My partner grabbed the night vision goggles on the dashboard and stuffed a handful of those annoying ass sunflower seeds back into his mouth.

"Do me a favor and remind me again. Who in the fuck are those two sitting in the Honda with their lights off?"

"That's our C.I. with the other suspect we've been looking for."

Detective Whitehead took the lid off his styrofoam coffee cup and spit the sunflower shells inside. He started to move his finger across the focusing wheel of the binoculars. "Why are we waiting here then? Let's go arrest those sons of bitches."

A smile stretched across my face so long you would've thought I was getting sucked off by a midget underneath the steering wheel. The difference between a seasoned vet like myself and a wet behind the ear newbie, was instead of rushing to the Honda to lock up one suspect, if we sit here and wait then we can watch the show and lock them all up.

Deshaun

Chapter 51

The mint green numbers holding steady on the digital clock above the dashboard read 12:23 am. We've been here for over an hour and no sign of Pernell yet. I knew Slim had to be tired of me asking if he was sure that Pernell was inside but I couldn't help myself. My mind was fixated on what needed to be done and the sooner we could do it, the better. P-Nutt's words kept playing in my head like a broken record. "There's not one nigga that is bigger than the set. We all can get it."

I was about to ask Slim for the eighteenth time if he was sure Pernell was in there but he tapped my leg then the double doors of the mansion swung open and I slid my body lower in my seat so only my eyes could see over the dash. Pernell stood outside the house, his back faced us and the security gate that kept him safe inside. Krystal stood in the center of the doorway, her arms wrapped themselves around her torso to keep her robe from exposing her pregnant belly.

I cranked the handle a good six times before the window was a quarter of the way down. Krystal's head was bobbing but I couldn't hear a word she was saying. Pernell just stood there, arms folded across his chest and head slightly cocked to the right listening to whatever the mother of his soon-to-be son had to say. Out of nowhere, Krystal's shoulders started heaving uncontrollably, her arms released their grip around her robe, exposing her belly. She reached toward Pernell for comfort but he swatted her arms to the ground.

Krystal's cry pierced through the cocoon of blackness the night provided like a hot knife to butter but her cries didn't faze Pernell one bit. He didn't even turn around to listen to anything she had to say. He just kept walking, walking down the driveway away from Krystal and away from his unborn seed.

The entrance of the iron gate was only forty yards ahead of where Slim and I had been parked for the last hour and a half, and when Pernell got to the entrance he hopped it like we did any other gate. Standing there with his face in his hands, his shoulders started doing the same thing Krystal's did before he slapped her hands away. Pernell looked like a shell of himself, his shoulders were no longer held up by his brazen bravado but were now sunken into his chest. His head glanced our way but if he noticed us he didn't care because he turned in the opposite direction and began walking.

Luckily I was built no bigger than a toothpick because I didn't need to open my door much more than the width of my fist to slip out. I flipped my hoodie over my head to blend in with as much of the darkness as possible. The .38 against my hip that Slim provided me was now an extension of my hand. The duct tape around the handle felt like stickum I used on my hands before a football game.

It was only weeks ago when Pernell and I walked side by side shooting the shit, bantering one another on who was going to steal the next bottle of liquor from Ralphs, and now I was behind him, stalking him as he taught me to do to others. The Sweetgum trees with their spiky green balls were beginning to drop their leaves onto the sidewalk, making it difficult to stay undetected.

Pernell wasn't following any of the advice he'd given me months previous. Not once did he check his surroundings while he marched forward, nor was he walking on the opposite side of the street. It felt like I was following a fighter taking his last walk away from the ring. Pernell had given up but I couldn't. My freedom depended on what I was going to do next.

Always be committed to your commitments, that was the oath, and now it was my time to make payment on it.

Pernell reached the end of the cul-de-sac near a row of neatly manicured Japanese Boxwood shrubs that flanked a one hoop basketball court to his right. The orange glow from the high-pressure sodium lamps above the court brought light to the face I haven't seen in weeks. They say we exchange youth for knowledge as time passes but perhaps Pernell was trading his health for his. His face that had been as fresh as any new tee from Fam Mart months ago now looked more like beef jerky, dried and somewhat leathery. His edge up, once meticulously manicured to keep his waves in their place, was now practically overgrown and for the most part turning into an afro.

By all means, Pernell was a shell of himself. He stood in the center of the court, his head tilted backward exposing his neck, his lips mumbling words that were hardly audible. Whatever he was whispering to God I no longer wanted to know. What he's done there's no excuse for. No one person is bigger than the set, not even my best friend.

I stood from behind the shrubs and aimed.

Pernell's voice finally traveled further than his lips. "How'd you find me D?"

My lips remained glued.

"Did buster ass Slim tell you where I was?"

I didn't answer. I just kept walking, keeping the barrel pointed at his nose.

"I know why they sent you but on Piru, it ain't what it seems."

My tongue couldn't be tamed anymore. Everything went red. My brain went in overdrive picking up every memory we built together over the last four months. There were just too many things that didn't make sense. We stood in the middle of the court and the barrel of my .38 only centimeters from Pernell's forehead. "Then what the fuck is it nigga? How did the babylons get the gun YOU said you would get rid of, huh? And how in the fuck do they have our conversation from the night at Krystal's house? Explain that shit to me, nigga!"

"Because, nigga." His voice trailed off as he cleared his throat. "Because Krystal gave 'em everything. She had the necklace she bought wired and it recorded all our conversations. Once they had me locked in the bounty they went to her pad and spooked her some more. They spooked her so much, she ended up taking them to the canyon where I buried the burners that night."

Shaking my head in disbelief my hand tightened around the .38 while I kept it pointed at his nose. Why would Krystal do some shit like that? Why would she jeopardize Pernell's freedom, the father of her child? I shook the hoodie off my head to get a clearer picture of Pernell. "If that's the case, then how in the fuck are you free, nigga?"

"Because, nigga. Krystal begged her father to bail me out. He's running for district attorney this year. He thinks since he bailed me out and she's carrying my son that I will turn state evidence to help him close this case and win the election. But fuck blood. I ain't never snitched and I ain't finna start now."

My eyes filled with embarrassment and my chin collapsed in my chest. How could I be so indoctrinated that I was willing to murder my best friend? Then I felt it. Pernell was pressing his forehead against the barrel. What the fuck was he doing? I tried pulling my arm away but his hand around my wrist was like a vise grip. The loose skin on his forehead between the barrel and his skull continued to move around in uneven circles.

"Shoot, D!"

"Hell nah, what the fuck are you doing?!"

"Pull the fucking trigger!"

"No."

He lodged his thumb in between the trigger guard and my index finger and started pressing. The pressure from his thumb felt like it was going to snap my finger in half. "You have to, D! There's no other choice. If the truth comes out that Krystal told, whatchu think is finna happen to her? Huh?"

Pernell was right. I hadn't thought of that.

"If you kill me, then Krystal's secret ends with me and our son breaks the cycle. Let me go out like a G, my nigga."

I kept trying to pull my arm back from Pernell's grip but I couldn't. The tips of my fingers were turning into a bed of needles. "I ain't shootin' you, Y.A.! Let my fuckin' wrist go!"

Pernell wrapped his other hand around my wrist and put another finger on top of his thumb. "Shoot, you bitch-ass nigga!"

My finger snapped.

Detective Braveheart

Chapter 52

Whitehead threw his binoculars in the backseat and turned to me. I could see that us sitting in the car not doing anything was bothering the shit out of him. "Do you see that shit?" He was pointing at a shadow being followed by another shadow. They were two hundred yards in front of us and our suspect, doing the following, made sure to keep a twenty-yard distance between himself and his target. I knew what was going on. I've been waiting on this since our C.I. called three days ago informing me he was picking up our last remaining suspect from the triple homicide on Labor Day.

I took the half empty bottle of Pepto-Bismol from my door panel and tossed it onto Whitehead's lap. "I told you to sit back and enjoy the show. It's about to get better."

"Fuck you Braveheart and your old man remedies."

Whitehead was clueless and that's how I liked it. The less he knew the more strings I could pull. My plan was coming together perfectly and Krystal's cooperation made all the pieces to the puzzle fit. Our C.I. was right when he said she will be an asset to our investigation and after tonight this will be my last shit show. These convictions should put me right over three hundred and position me for the captain's desk when he retires next month. After fifteen years of locking up these dumb-ass niggers it's time for me to kick my feet up and reap the benefits of taxpayer dollars. Buttoning up this triple homicide will do just that.

Whitehead picked up the Pepto-Bismol, swished it around his mouth like listerine and scooted closer to the dash. His eyes were trying to make out what I already knew happened. He pointed at the last man standing. Even though I'm the one pulling the strings I still can't believe everything came together so perfectly. There's no fucking way they could take the Captain spot from me now. I was the sure pick and Whitehead must've known it too. "So this was the show I was supposed to watch, huh?"

"What the fuck were you expecting Whitehead? Some Dick Tracy movie shit? This is real fucking life! Shit needs to get done out here and I make sure it does. Not you, not the Cap, not the dumb-ass beat cops who don't know shit. It's me! I clean these streets up." I took the 9mm out of my holster and racked the slide. "Quit being a pussy and let's go!"

Deshaun

Chapter 53

This couldn't be happening. Yes, I was supposed to kill Pernell but not like this. Not with him pressing my finger to do so. I was here to knock him off because we thought he was a snitch, not because he wanted to be a martyr and save Krystal and his unborn seed. What he did was real love, that was the same love he preached to me about having for the set. Pernell would protect anyone and help anyone because that's the type of love he had for the homies and the set. As long as you were all in, he was all in with you.

My eyes were stuck looking at Pernell's face pressed against the asphalt below me. Tiny white pebbles of gravel were scattered across his forehead and implanted to his blood-soaked face. His eyelids that were a bit oversized for his face were now pinned behind the skin underneath his eyebrows. Taking my palm I slid it across his face. "Rest in paradise, Pernell. I promise I will clear all this shit up. On Piru."

"Freeze you piece of shit! Or I will blow your fucking brains out!" My body went stiff. How in the fuck are the police already here? It hasn't been but five

322

minutes since Pernell used my finger to kill himself. There weren't even any sirens. "I told you I was going to get your black ass. It was only a matter of time."

His voice finally registered. This was the same GSU detective that roughed me up after I got jumped in front of the liquor store with Sky. He's the one who threw me against the fence and slammed me on the sidewalk after they took me to my uncle's house. He's the one who applied his knee so hard on the back of my head that my nose began to bleed on the concrete. He was the one who pressed his department-issued 9mm so hard against the back of my skull that I couldn't sleep with my head on the back of my pillow for a month. He's the one who said if I move, he'd kill me.

I snatched the .38 lying next to Pernell's chest and swung around. This time my trigger finger didn't need any pressure from an outside source, it kept squeezing until the kick against my wrist stopped. From behind the bushes, there wasn't any more movement. It was silent except for the ringing in my ears. Then the flashes came. One after another. The first shot buzzed by my ear and chipped away at the gravel five feet ahead of me. I jumped over Pernell and tried sprinting to the other side of the court. Then I heard three more.

I kept running but my legs had their own idea and my body slid across the asphalt. Something ripped through my lower back above my kidneys. There was no pain, just a sudden impact that left my lower half inoperable. I tried using my elbows like an ice pick to pull me forward but it felt like I was trying to pull a tank across the sand.

Another bullet whizzed by and shattered a chunk of asphalt onto my face. Then I felt a shadow hovering over me. "I told your nigger ass I was going to be the motherfucker to bury you!" His southern drawl made his words sound sticky as molasses. He used his boot to roll me onto my back. Behind the barrel of the 9mm was a smile that stretched from ear to ear across his red face. "Say goodnight, nigger!"

I closed my eyes and took one last breath. It wasn't supposed to end like this but honestly, I didn't know how it was supposed to end. In four months, I've been part of so much carnage. Why did I expect anything different for me? P-Nutt warned me that day at the park when I got put on, that death or prison came with all this, but I thought I was the exception to the rule. I thought because I just started bangin' I had time, that those things like death and prison only happened to people who have been active for a while. But I guess I was wrong. When you're bangin' you never know when your last breath will be. I opened my eyes and stared at the blue eyed devil standing over me. "Fuck you, you bitch-ass babylon. Do what the fuck you gotta do."

Jennifer Brown

Chapter 54

It's not over until my God says it's over! Deshaun has been a fighter since I gave birth to him, and right now will be no different. He didn't die when his little heart was three times bigger than any normal infant, so he ain't about to die now. Screw what the doctors think. They ain't God. God is the only one that can say if Deshaun's time is up or not.

They wouldn't even let me see my baby. They had the audacity to call security on me when all I did was politely push the nurse out of my way. If she didn't have two left feet, she wouldn't have fallen on her flat behind. That's not my fault. That's what I was explaining to the security when they escorted me out of the lobby. But that wasn't all. What made matters worse was getting home and seeing what the police, whose salary I pay with my damn tax dollars, have done to our apartment.

We don't deserve to be treated like we're one of these suspects on that ridiculous show, Cops, where they ransack the house for no good reason. I don't care what they're saying about my baby. We didn't raise a murderer. He wouldn't hurt a fly, and I mean literally.

When he was 12 years old, he and his friends, Alex and Lee, went so far as to make a fly trap that attracted flies in a biodegradable container so that they wouldn't have to kill them. Deshaun believed every creature had the right to live, which was God's gift to us all. What kind of murderer is going to do something like that? Not any that I've seen on TV and I watch a lot of it.

What the police did in Deshaun's room didn't make any sense at all. Everything was everywhere: clothes, pictures, trophies. It didn't matter. Whatever they put their hands on was now on the carpet. They even kicked over his dresser like it had done something wrong.

Whatever they thought they were looking for, sure wasn't in this house because his father and I made sure of it. After I took him to the Greyhound we cleaned that place like the Pope was coming to stay the night. That's when I stumbled across the journal I bought him for his fourteenth birthday, it was duct taped to the inside panel of his dresser. I knew something wasn't adding up. Deshaun never kept secrets from me anymore. That was our promise with one another after the incident at Admiral Baker's house when his wife informed me that he, Alex and Lee were caught playing "hide and go get it" with their triplet daughters. After that, he promised he would never keep anything from me again.

His journal was filled with entries that sounded like they were directly out of those rap songs he started listening to once we moved over here. And that boy who's now dead. The one the police are saying Deshaun killed. The one who I told Deshaun I didn't trust.

Pernell! That's right. That's what his name was.

He's to blame for all this, not Deshaun. My baby was just trying to fit in and that boy manipulated him. It says it all throughout Deshaun's journal, I know how to read between the lines. My son wasn't a thief before we moved here. That boy forced Deshaun into stealing alcohol from those stores. He was also the kid who told Deshaun to meet him at that park, from what I'm reading, and that was the first night Deshaun stayed out past his curfew. I knew that boy was no good. Deshaun is not the monster the police are trying to make him out to be. He was only doing what that boy forced him to do. And if he did kill anybody, it's probably because he was protecting himself.

Let me check my answering machine. The doctor said they will call once he got out of surgery.

Deshaun

Chapter 55

◆◆◆

In a matter of four months, everything changed. No longer was I a naive kid living in the suburbs planning his senior trip with his best friends. Now I'm laying in the hospital wishing I would've died on the basketball court with Pernell, rather than wondering what was going to happen to me next.

The nurse's warm purple latex hand checked the area around the bag that was connected to my stomach. "Excuse me, ma'am, how long have I been here?" She looked up at me but didn't say a word. Her face was uncaring, like I was some sort of scumbag that didn't deserve a breath to be wasted on. The disinfectant rubbed along the floors in the hallway by the janitor's dirty mops filled my nose. Other than the beeping sound from the rectangular box next to me the room was silent.

I reached to rub my eyes to get a better visual of my surroundings but my wrists were shackled to the metal rail that wrapped around my hospital bed. How the fuck was I the one shot but handcuffed? Where the fuck do they think I'm running to right now, home?

Yeah right, I can't even lift myself up off this hospital bed.

The noise outside of my room caught my attention. If the room had windows I wouldn't have had to strain to listen to the voices outside my door. "Doc, how long will he be hospitalized?"

"Two more weeks should do it and then he's all yours, detectives."

My eyes were glued shut, hoping the detectives didn't notice I was awake. "Why in the fuck didn't you call that shit in? I'm not losing my badge over your cowboy bullshit!"

Detective Braveheart's familiar drawl grabbed my attention. My hearing was the only thing that was operating at a hundred percent. "Don't act fucking dumb now. You know why I didn't call this shit in, partner. If I had, then Internal Affairs would be all up in our asses by now. They would want to know why we were there in the first place. And you know what that means, right?"

"No, I don't. So please tell me, Mr. I Do What The Fuck I Want."

That same chuckle I heard before he fired that last shot filled my ears again, "You just don't get it, huh? If I would have called this in, that would mean we would've had to leak our confidential informants, and that's something I don't fucking do, detective!"

Confidential informants? What the fuck is he talking about? I thought Krystal was the only one telling. Who else is fucking telling?